T0129398

COOKING
& SCREAMING

COOKING
& SCREAMING

Adrienne Kane

Simon Spotlight Entertainment

New York   London   Toronto   Sydney

SSE

Simon Spotlight Entertainment
A Division of Simon & Schuster, Inc.
1230 Avenue of the Americas
New York, NY 10020

First Simon Spotlight Entertainment hardcover edition February 2009

SIMON SPOTLIGHT ENTERTAINMENT and colophon are trademarks
of Simon & Schuster, Inc.

For information about special discounts for bulk purchases,
please contact Simon & Schuster Special Sales at 1-800-456-6798 or
business@simonandschuster.com

Designed by C. Linda Dingler

Manufactured in the United States of America

10 9 8 7 6 5 4 3 2 1

Library of Congress Cataloging-in-Publication Data

Kane, Adrienne.
   Cooking and screaming: finding my own recipe for recovery / Adrienne
Kane.
      p. cm.
   Includes bibliographical references and index.
   1. Kane, Adrienne—Health. 2. Fistula, Arteriovenous—Patients—
California—Biography. 3. Cooks—California—Biography. I. Title.
   RC776.A6K36 2008
   641.5092—dc22
   [B]   2008043245

ISBN-13: 978-1-4767-3900-7

for my mother and my sister

Contents

Contents

COOKING
& SCREAMING

CHAPTER 1

Tagliatelle with Grated Zucchini

Pasta. Nourishing, quick, easy, and wholly satisfying. I practically lived off the stuff in college. This recipe has remained one of the vestiges of my college days, with good reason. The zucchini becomes an altogether different vegetable upon grating—as velvety and sumptuous as any vegetable can become.

2 tablespoons unsalted butter
1 tablespoon olive oil
1 small dried chili, like chili d'arbol, or a healthy pinch of red pepper flakes
2 ½ cups grated zucchini
2 cloves garlic, thinly sliced
salt and pepper to taste
½ cup heavy cream
8 ounces dried tagliatelle pasta
¼ cup minced fresh flat-leaf parsley
½ cup grated Parmesan cheese
¼–½ cup reserved pasta cooking water

In a large skillet, over medium heat, melt the butter and olive oil. Crumble the chili and sauté briefly. Turn the heat to medium-high and add the zucchini, garlic, salt, and pepper, tossing to combine. The zucchini should be glossy and completely coated in the butter and olive oil. Flatten into a large pancake so that the zucchini begins to exude liquid. Continue sautéing and flattening for 8–10 minutes, until the liquid is gone and the zucchini begins to brown and has reduced in volume by a third.

Add the heavy cream and bring to a simmer. Reduce the heat to low and cook for 1–2 minutes, allowing the flavors to marry. Meanwhile cook the pasta according to the package instructions until al dente. Toss the pasta with the sauce. Add the parsley, cheese, and any of the pasta cooking water that might be needed to make the sauce loose and flowing. Taste for seasoning and serve with extra Parmesan cheese.

serves 2, with leftovers

Baby Food

had been eating a lot of pasta lately, in all of its many forms. As college life got busier, my meals became increasingly brief, tossed together with ease, eaten, and oftentimes forgotten.

Through the back windows in my kitchen, the sun illuminated the pile of dishes resting in the sink. I *will* get to those, I thought. I had been a bit frantic lately; my rear end had seemed fused to my desk chair as I spent hours in front of my computer working on my thesis. The end was in sight; this life of imminent papers and stacks of textbooks was coming to a close. My days as a student were coming to a close.

It was a tome, or at least it was in my narrow, nearly postcollegiate world. I left the warmth of the kitchen, and walking to my desk, pulled the final pages of my paper from the printer, neatly placing them into the stack. I grew proud and hungry. Grabbing a bowl of pasta I had made the night before, I took a seat on the floor. I was surprised by my eagerness to lunch on leftovers. But this tagliatelle was one of my favorites. There are certain foods that take on a different identity when reheated, one that makes them exciting and new, if those adjectives can even be used to describe a bowl of pasta. This pasta was blanketed in a pale, creamy green sauce, like a light pesto, but with the smooth, luxurious flavor of another pasta altogether. In the moment's respite I had the night before, I stood grating zucchini into piles of shaggy shards. The vegetable had nearly melted, and its traces, combined with a splash of cream, turned the contents of the pan into a sumptuous sauce. By the next day, the pasta grew drier, soaking up the cream and leaving behind bits of fiery chili while the zucchini clung steadfastly to each noodle.

I slurped, then chewed. In my right hand was my senior thesis, "The Memoir as a Means to Freudian Psychoanalysis as Seen in Nabokov's *Speak, Memory*." I had loved this book, voluntarily becoming lost in Nabokov's language for these final weeks of college. My life had become a to and fro, stripped down to the bare essentials. Days were spent in the modern dance studio; in the evenings, I would hunker down in my apartment, curling up on my couch with my dog-eared copy of *Speak, Memory* and stacks of Freudian reference books.

I had just enough time to put my pasta bowl in the sink, grab a sweater to ward off the chill of Berkeley in the late spring, and meet Maia, my best friend, who had diligently agreed to give my thesis a final read before I turned it in.

I hopped into the car, making my way down the hill to the flatlands near the university. I passed the elementary school, the playground empty and swing set still on this Sunday afternoon.

Cooking & Screaming

Letting my elbow rest on the open car window, I allowed the cool breezes of May in the Bay Area to mingle with the car's stale air. The wisteria were in bloom, the lavender vines drooping heavily along the entrance to a stately brick church near my apartment. Farther down the hill, the Greene and Greene house, an emblem of the Arts and Crafts movement, with its oxidized copper trim and pagoda-esque eaves, stood alongside the frat houses, ramshackle, littered with beer bottles, and lawn furniture poised on the roof. Berkeley had become my home. It was a place where I was given the opportunity to encounter a variety of different people.

Sitting next to the grubby college student, the politically active classmate, the jocks, and the theater people in giant lecture halls, I steered my way through these countless niches but never truly found my own. Being at Berkeley was as much about a solid college education as it was a place to try on identities. It was difficult to find the ideal, but I *had* discovered a few things about myself along the way. I loved to dance; I could curl up with a good book for hours; and nothing was more restorative to me than a home-cooked meal. I was young and unencumbered. Living in Berkeley offered me the freedom of endless possibilities. But these endless possibilities also kept me wide-eyed in the middle of the night, raising the question: What do I want to do with the rest of my life?

Maia met me on the corner of Haste and Telegraph, right near Amoeba Records, which was blaring a forgotten hit from the sixties. Over the past four years, I had spent countless Sunday afternoons there, thumbing through the overstuffed racks while some ultraobscure band played in the background.

Maia was punctual as usual, and we walked to get a cup of coffee near campus. Prattling on about our weekends, we traveled arm in arm, as we often did, creating a barrier against the students stumbling home single-mindedly during finals week. Introduced through a mutual friend, Maia and I had become fast friends when we both stayed to enjoy Berkeley in the summertime. When the students go home for their break, Berkeley becomes a ghost town, and Maia and I enjoyed the quiet. I am not sure if it comes from the warm weather, or maybe it is the length of the days, but everything seems to move at warp speed during the summer months. Maia and I had many late-night talks and shared many evenings cooking elaborate meals for no one but the two of us. Now, almost two years later, she had agreed to proofread my thesis, despite the craze of finals week for her as well. Maia was so articulate, even her slang was grammatically correct.

Telegraph Avenue, the main street leading toward UC Berkeley, offers an odd assortment of typical college town shops, bookstores, and retailers selling "Cal gear," mixed in with the unsavory sort of tattoo parlors, tobacco emporiums with giant hookahs in the window, and ancient Mexican restaurants serving grilled burritos. I had traveled these blocks so many times that it seemed the sidewalks had grown accustomed to my footprint. Maia and I pushed our way past rows of vendors selling tie-dyed T-shirts toward Wall Berlin, the leftist coffeehouse that had the blackest coffee. We were only blocks away when I casually mentioned that I didn't feel well.

Suddenly my vision narrowed. My surroundings were spinning, my mouth went bone-dry, and my stomach felt as if I had ridden on a rickety carnival roller coaster after consuming too many corn dogs. So I sat down on the curb of Telegraph Avenue. Littered with trash and cigarette butts, smelling of a mixture of urine and patchouli-scented incense, Telegraph Avenue is not a place where anyone should be sitting, let alone lying down, yet I then assumed a prone position. As Maia watched me drift off, my body beginning to go limp on the sidewalk, she called 911. Moments later, the ambulance came and she rode with me to the hospital, preparing to make the phone call that no one ever wants to make.

It wasn't one of those phone calls that wake a mother in the middle of the night, when the ringing of the phone at 3:00 A.M. signals doom, but that phone call, alerting my mother that her youngest daughter was taken to the hospital at 4:00 P.M., was met with the same amount of dread. Maia told my mother that she had gotten me to the hospital, that I wasn't feeling well, that the doctors hadn't told her anything yet. My mother told my father to stay at home and wait for her call. "I'm sure everything is fine," she said, and then she left to pick up my sister Jennifer, who was living only fifteen minutes away.

It had always been just my sister and me. She was six years my senior, and from the time that I could walk, I trotted around behind Jennifer. I idolized her, even through those gawky middle school years. Even with the pain of bad haircuts and elasticized shorts, I thought that she was beautiful. When Jennifer was driving in high school, I looked forward to her picking me up after school, the latest New Wave band blaring out of the speaker of her petite Ford Tempo. That May day, she made the drive over the Bay Bridge to the East Bay with my mother. It seemed that everyone was out for a Sunday drive, as my grandma used to say.

7

Adrienne Kane

A trip that should have taken forty-five minutes turned into an anxious two-hour journey. As they drove, I weaved in and out of consciousness. My recollections of that day are spotty. I do not remember the whirling lights of the ambulance, or Maia making the call to my parents' house, or calling my boyfriend, Brian, who also rushed to the hospital. In fact, I recall little besides the large white ceiling tiles that hung above my gurney when I first arrived at the hospital. I remained in this semiconscious state until my mother arrived and announced to me that she was there. Reaching under the tightly fitted hospital sheets, she grasped my hand and squeezed as only a mother can do, her presence allowing me to bow out gracefully. I tumbled into unconsciousness and remained that way for three weeks.

I HADN'T BEEN to the hospital since birth. No broken bones, never a stitch, no nothing. My childhood days were spent trying to emulate Jennifer or taking dance classes. Things might have been different if I had fallen off a bike or smacked my head on a diving board—or had any number of typical suburban kid accidents. Perhaps I would have been rushed to the hospital, wheeled into the MRI machine, and the doctors would have detected *it*—the slight malformation in my brain, the tangle of arteries, a little knot inside the labyrinth of gray matter, biding its time, and waiting to burst.

An AVM, arterio-venous malformation, is quite a mouthful. I remember asking my family to repeat to me what I had suffered. "AVM, AVM, arterio-venous what?" At night, when I couldn't sleep, I repeated those initials over and over to myself, hoping

8

that in the morning I would actually remember them. But I did not, could not, for several weeks. The AVM had left me with a deficit in speech and cognition, as well as complete paralysis of my right side.

There are two kinds of strokes. The more common is the ischemic variety, a clot in a blood vessel. Then there is the hemorrhagic, or the bleeding sort. An AVM is the latter. Inside the brain is a mess of capillaries. Their main function is to distribute the blood around the brain, into its tiniest recesses. Without them, we would be what I like to call a nonfunctioning blood head. In most people, these capillaries are well-developed conduits, but for two to five in every thousand people, they are not. For those people, the capillary walls are malformed, and occasionally, without warning, they rupture, seeping blood into the precious matter that is the human brain. The result can be either death or symptoms similar to stroke: paralysis, slurred speech, memory loss, obstructed vision, and so on. Guess who happened to be a part of that small percentage? I never win anything. But when it comes to AVMs, I struck the jackpot.

There is an astounding unpredictability to AVMs. Some people live their entire life with one and don't even know it. It may even rupture and the person may never know. Doctors have yet to determine the whys or whens. The effect of an AVM depends on its location. Mine was in the basal ganglia region, an area deep within the brain that controls both fine and gross motor skills.

WHEN I REGAINED consciousness, weeks had passed. Wires and plugs twisted off my bed like vines winding their way up a trellis, and the blipping of monitors blended with the nurses' conversations in the hallway. The brevity of a northern California spring had come and gone. Like a wisp, I had missed it.

Those initial weeks were ones of slumber for me. My eyelids were like lead and I could only force them open for a few minutes each day. Doctors would nudge me into wakefulness, shining pinpoint flashlights into my eyes and forcing me to answer simple questions, like what day of the week it was. They would gather around my bed awaiting my answer. As I would reply, my voice would crackle. And as I eventually became more lucid, the questions got slightly more challenging. The doctors soon gave me the all clear to eat with abandon, secure that I could manage by myself, and snacking is what I most enjoyed. First, there was snack food: a small pile of cheese-flavored crackers; a short stack of saddle-shaped, original-flavored Pringles, cradled neatly one on top of another; and bits and bites of an assorted box of milk chocolates. Each lay in a loose pile on my chest. They would go on rotation. A cheese cracker, leaving a dusty orange trail on my hospital gown, was followed by a crumble of dehydrated potato, then a nibble of chocolate, another chocolate morsel, the crisp crackle of a cracker, and so on. I requested Doritos from one visitor, peanut butter from another, chocolate sandwich cookies from yet another. The windowsill of my hospital room looked like the aisle of a convenience store. Still confined to my bed, I would request a small pile of snacks to be laid on my chest. My mother was only too happy to comply, and the nurses would snicker at the skinny girl's feast.

All of my senses had become muted. I couldn't quite see straight—I had to wear an eye patch, like a pirate's matey. My speech was jilted. Hearing wavered in and out of pitch. And food tasted different—it, too, seemed somehow muted. Which must be why I loved and requested junk food so much. I could clearly see the bright orange of the cracker, hear the crunch of the fried potatoes, and savor the sweetness of the chocolate as it slipped down my throat. No one eats cheese crackers for the subtlety of flavor. It was as if I needed that sodium, those ingredients I couldn't pronounce, to know what food was *supposed* to taste like.

GROWING UP, MY mom packed well-balanced lunches for me. Other kids would buy prepared foods—the latest pizza pocket or a frozen burrito—and zap them in the school's microwave; I was never allowed. Out of my brown paper sack I would pull a turkey sandwich, two veggies, a piece of fruit, and some cookies. It wasn't that sweets were banned altogether; it was just that the rest of the meal had to be nutritious.

Once a month, I was allowed certain sugar cereals. And I would wait all month long for that precious visit to the grocery store. Standing in the vast cereal aisle for what seemed like hours, I would try to select the choice box of cereal: one that was sugary but not dyed neon hues (those were never allowed), one that would sweeten the milk in the cereal bowl but not leave it a murky slick, a cereal that kept the right consistency in milk—not too crisp, not mushy. When the ideal box was agreed upon, I waited eagerly until we got home from the market to pour the perfect bowl. That first sugary bite of longed-for cereal came with such a feeling of pure, unadulterated happiness—like waking up at noon on a Saturday well rested after a long week of getting up early for school.

So I guess it's no wonder that the first thing I craved in the hospital was junk food. As much as the desire for processed cheese snacks was about finding a morsel of flavor strong enough to break through my new muted world, I was also in pursuit of that same happiness, that same gleeful feeling of having your first bite of something new. Little did I know how many new culinary adventures awaited me in the next phase of recovery.

CHAPTER 2

Cantor Cohen's Noodle Kugel

For many, casseroles are part of their culinary lexicon. They just weren't for me. Except for kugel. Kugel is a traditional Eastern European Jewish dish, and although most of the ingredients are sweet, it is not served as a dessert. Rather, this dish is a complement to savory meals, like brisket. This recipe is from a yellowed-with-age spiral-bound cookbook from the first temple that my parents belonged to, written by the cantor of that temple's family. Made on special occasions, kugel had been the only casserole in my culinary lexicon—that is, until I began my tenure at the hospital in Vallejo.

1 pound wide egg noodles
(cooked according to
package directions)
1 cup sugar
1 pound cottage cheese
1½ teaspoons vanilla extract
4 ounces (1 stick) melted
unsalted butter, plus
additional to grease
the pan

1 cup golden raisins
7 eggs
2 ½–3 cups milk
1 pint sour cream

FOR THE TOPPING:
½ cup crumbled cornflakes
1 teaspoon cinnamon
1 teaspoon sugar

Mix together all of the kugel ingredients except the topping mixture and place in a 9 × 13 inch greased Pyrex pan. Refrigerate overnight to thicken and meld the flavors.

Preheat the oven to 350°F. Before baking the kugel, mix the topping ingredients together. Sprinkle the topping over the kugel, then dot with additional butter. Bake for approximately 1½ hours, or until golden on top. Check during the last 15 minutes to make sure the kugel is not baking too fast and getting too brown. If it is beginning to brown too quickly, cover it with aluminum foil. The kugel is ready when it is heated through and bubbly. Wait approximately 10 minutes before dishing up.

serves 18

Test Kitchen

I **don't remember having** any conversations with my doctors, family, or friends about what had happened to me. I just sort of knew. Knew that I was paralyzed, knew that I had no mobility on the right side of my body. The one thing I did not know is what my fate would be and the seemingly endless road that lay ahead of me. When I was first moved from my hospital bed, I was presented with a wheelchair as my new mode of transportation. I hated that wheelchair. I detested the fact that every time I glanced into the mirror, the girl wearing the eye patch staring back at me was unrecognizable. I was in need of a haircut, my skin was sallow and greasy, I was gaunt from being fed intravenously for weeks, and the right side of my face literally drooped. It looked as if I had had a reverse face-lift. The person reflected back at me was unfamiliar. Mirrors are kept hidden for a reason in hospitals; it can be shocking to see how someone really looks while recuperating. The stiff hospital gown was not my clothing,

the greenish cast of the fluorescent hospital lights was less than
flattering, and the girl with hanging limbs was me. I had entered
a new territory.

I had always kept mostly to myself. My days most recently had
been filled with lectures and dance classes, and I looked forward
to my time alone. I would chat with my fellow dancers before
we would take our places at the barre. We would smile and nod
while tying on our pointe shoes. But after class, while some dancers would stand, stretching their hamstrings, flexing their feet,
and talking to one another, I would duck out. It was never that
I would stop dancing as soon as I left the classroom—quite the
opposite. Back in my apartment, sitting down to a bowl of hot
soup, I would mentally rehearse the choreography in my head
and think about improvements for the next class. But now, in the
hospital, I was never alone. There was always a family member
or a close friend, a doctor or a nurse, or at times both. Now I always needed someone there. It was as if the company warded off
the demons and kept me from asking the truly terrifying question: When would I be well again?

My senior year of college was the year of Dionne Warwick for
me. Not the "That's What Friends Are For" Dionne Warwick, but
the Burt Bacharach Dionne. I had discovered her thirty years too
late. And I loved her: the cat's-eye eyeliner, the bouffant hairdos,
the raspy vocals. She sang of suburban love lost, which I couldn't
relate to, but I adored her nonetheless. It was Dionne who would
first sing to me in my hospital bed. Brian, my boyfriend, had been
told that patients may need a little bit of home to curtail the hospital monotony. He slipped a set of headphones over my ears one
night shortly after I woke up, and there was that beautiful raw

voice, singing to me. I teared up instantly. Who knows—maybe it was the massive amounts of drugs coursing through my veins at that moment, or maybe it was the emotion in her voice.

Three weeks in the ICU and I was given the option to go home or to go to another intensive rehabilitation hospital. Obviously, returning home was the more attractive proposition—my own bed, my mother's cooking, and a community of family and friends on which to lean. But I knew that the rehabilitation hospital was the wiser option. It provided intensive physical therapy, hands-on occupational therapy, and a team of doctors monitoring my every move. So I went to the wasteland of Vallejo, California, overrun with mini-malls and fast-food chains, about one and a half hours outside of San Francisco, to get "rehabilitated."

The rehabilitation hospital in Vallejo can best be described as a perverse summer camp for adults. Yes, a summer camp, but without any feeling of community and definitely no laying around the pool to escape the sweltering heat. There were, however, passels of physical therapists barking commands and excitedly giving words of encouragement, much like camp counselors. The patients-cum-campers were the pleasers, the sulkers, the criers, the sweat-ers, the screamers, and the easily excitables, all thrown together, doing what we were told, but with a healthy dose of skepticism. My cabin was a room with three other women, all with neurological disorders of their own. One, a grandmother who had suffered a stroke; another, a middle-aged housewife with a degenerative neurological ailment, wheeling around in an enormous motorized wheelchair; and finally, a gunshot victim who had been paralyzed from the waist down. But I was by far the youngest. There was no competition, but there was also no camaraderie. Unlike summer camp, there were no late-night gab sessions. When we came back to the room after a long day of physical therapy, the curtains were drawn by the nurses, keeping each roommate to herself until bedtime. The evenings were silent, save for the murmuring din of each roommate's individual television set.

A feeling of desperation, and at times defeat, was pervasive. I was thrown together with other invalids, each with the knowledge of what they once were like—parents, teachers, businesspeople, doctors, handymen, and so on—and where they wanted to be again. But I did not feel sorry for anyone. Much like my fellow roommates, I was too tired and too busy to feel much of anything.

ALONE WE SLEPT, alone we rehabilitated, and—I was surprised to find—alone we ate. I have never been a solitary eater. Nor have I been a closet eater. There are some foods, aesthetically, that I prefer to eat alone. For instance, when eating crab—tearing off the claws with a pop, cracking the hard exterior, fish juice flying everywhere, and drawn butter dripping down your forearm—I would prefer a bit of privacy. But if you give me a soft-shelled crab, a clean napkin, and rousing conversation, I will be a happy diner.

Eating and preparing food is best enjoyed as a communal activity. Growing up, dinners were always shared around the kitchen table. And unless the presidential debates were happening or something particularly riveting was being aired on *60 Minutes*, we never ate in front of the TV set. But at Vallejo, the meals were brought in by the nurses on Melmac trays whose colors mirrored the linoleum tiles of the floor. A popular dinner combination was a watery bowl of vegetable soup with a few alphabet pasta noodles floating on top, paired with a mushy hamburger, the bun so large it mushroomed over the gray meat patty. At precisely 5:30 each evening, I was expected to flip on the television and eat my meal quietly, trying to ignore my roommates until bedtime, when the lights would go out and I would turn in for the night.

I HAD BEEN transported to Vallejo by ambulance, groggy and tired. It didn't bother me that I could only see the interior walls of the ambulance; tucked firmly into the gurney, I felt safe rather than claustrophobic. I knew where I was going. In fact, I had been there several years before. When I was seventeen, my father had suffered a massive stroke and was sent to this very hospital for rehabilitation. Back then, my weekends were spent driving to Vallejo and giving Dad an update about what was going on in the world that surrounded him. So, I guess you could say my family is rather unlucky when it comes to vascular health.

When the ambulance stopped and the EMTs wheeled the gurney outside, I hardly cared to move my head. I stared skyward, amazed by the hazy sunshine. I had been indoors for nearly one month. I had missed graduation. The last time I was outside was in the balmy, cool temperature of springtime by the bay, still needing a jacket in the mornings and evenings. Now it was hot enough to make perspiration bead along my hairline. As the EMTs wheeled me toward my destination, I focused on the concrete hospital towers and the seething cerulean sky.

It felt as though I had sprinted those ninety miles to Vallejo. I was physically exhausted and my right side hung heavy. The only way that I could move the right side of my body was with the left, grabbing my right arm and flinging it aside. I was brought to my bed and introduced to the afternoon nurse, a cheery woman with a booming voice and long cornrows, wearing fuchsia pink scrubs. My mother and the nurse helped me to bed. I closed my eyes for a moment, taking a deep breath, filling my lungs with the stale hospital air, and I didn't wake for several hours.

"Hi . . . Adrienne is it? I'm Donna; I'll be your speech therapist. I have some food for you. We just want to see how you can handle solids so that the hospital knows what kinds of meals to prepare for you." Little did she know that I had been eating hearty meals of junk food for weeks before being transferred to Vallejo.

Blinking slowly, I strained to focus on the rotund middle-aged woman standing at the foot of my bed and smiling at me. Disheveled, she was pulling at the hem of her short-sleeved polyblend blouse. Her look, though clearly thrown together, was one so warm, her manner so gentle, that I was immediately put at ease. After being examined by a litany of egotistical doctors and poked at by overzealous nurses, it seemed that each person I encountered at hospitals over the past weeks wanted something different from me. Just a little vial of my blood. Just to answer these few questions. But here was a woman who actually wanted something utterly simple from me, to see me eat a midafternoon snack; surely I could oblige. Then she unveiled the tray of food. I glanced at the dish, presealed and tidy in Tupperware. It didn't look very appetizing, but it was hard to determine what was appetizing anymore. With any sort of brain trauma, it is as if the slate has been wiped clean. Your body and your brain are out of sync; signals that normally feel like hunger or pain, reception to heat or cold, are decreased or eliminated entirely.

Now it seemed that everyone was offering me some type of get-well food or drink. Before being transferred to Vallejo, my uncle stopped to visit me in the hospital. Now a burly mountain man living with his partner near Yosemite, in a previous life he had been a chef in the Bay Area. With a penchant for collecting, he had stopped by an Asian shop near the hospital, buying yet another beautiful gilded fan to add to his increasing collection. Into my hospital room he crept, fan in one hand and cafe mocha in the other. He twirled around with the fan, doing a modest dance, and, pushing up the sleeves on his well-worn plaid flannel shirt, offered me a sip of the coffee. It looked and smelled so delicious, how could I refuse? That coffee was a distant apparition in those first weeks of slipping in and out of consciousness. Now, I peered down at the container, giving my newly naked, patchless eye a moment to adjust, and then back up at Donna.

"It's just a little snack; you don't have to eat it all. We want to see how you do."

"What is it?" I asked, my voice crackling with trepidation.

"Well." Donna picked up the lid, the condensation from the warm food dripping off the top and landing in a puddle on the tray. She took her index finger and used her hot-pink pearlescent polished fingernails to point, proclaiming, "You have a pizza casserole, some cooked green beans, and chocolate cake with cookie crumb topping!" She looked at me expectantly.

Pizza casserole? What the hell is pizza casserole? I'm a Jew. From California. Except for a dairy-rich noodle kugel, served at Rosh Hashanah, I had never consumed a casserole. I was familiar with the concept—a one-pot meal that is thrown together with ease—but what Donna was asking me to try was far from the

21

kugel that my mother made. Much like the beef brisket made for the same holiday, which had been braised then stewed for hours in a rich tomatoey broth until no knife was needed to slice into a morsel, kugel was a daylong process. It seemed like pounds of dairy products were released into the giant mixing bowl with the egg noodles before my mom set the concoction in the refrigerator in order to meld the flavors. I would peek in the refrigerator to see how the kugel was doing, longing to taste from the slippery, creamy casserole dish when it was baked the next day. But tuna noodle, chicken mushroom, broccoli cheese, and now pizza casserole were things with which I was unfamiliar.

In middle school, I had a close friend, Bethanny Brown. For lack of a more apt description, she was a WASP. In fact, it seemed the very acronym was created to define her family. Her father came home each night to their prim cottage-style home and was met by Bethanny's mother at the door, waiting to take his coat and hand him a scotch and soda. Dinners were eaten in the dining room; the kitchen table was saved for breakfast. And Bethanny's mother, who dabbled in substitute teaching, taped *Days of Our Lives* every weekday so that she could watch the program with her daughter after school.

One winter break, I went on a road trip with the Browns to southern California. Bethanny's mother packed a bottle of scotch for her dad, snack foods for us, and groceries, as we would be staying in a condo in Palm Springs upon our arrival and she would be doing the cooking. Unbeknownst to me, hidden away under the packaged stuffing mix and behind the can of pineapple rings was a canned ham, waiting to be served as dinner one night. After an exhausting day of Marco Polo in the swimming pool of the condo complex, Bethanny and I came inside, awaiting dinner. And there it was, naked, pink, and compressed—*the ham.* The quivering mass was set on a Pyrex dish, pierced with aromatic cloves, and adorned with sugary rings of yellow pineapple. Slices were passed around, and remembering what my mother told me about being polite, about at least trying all the foods that were set before me on this vacation, I took a slice. I watched each person at the table enjoy that ham, Bethanny's father eating with such gusto that he even had seconds. Meanwhile, I choked down that smooth meat product. Even the pineapple rings were unpleasant; they, too, had been tinged with meat juice. After that fateful meal, I couldn't eat ham, even the honey-baked sort, for years.

And now here was this pizza casserole, which I knew that I had to eat, to at least show the doctors that I was ready for solid food. I stared at this strange concoction of noodles and tomato sauce, garnished with a slice of melted mozzarella and topped with lubricous pepperoni slices. Pools of grease had settled in the shallow baked curves of meat. And I choked it down. It wasn't terrible, but it was unequivocally bad. Still I chewed and swallowed several times like a good girl. Yes, I could tolerate solid foods once more.

CHAPTER 3

Bolognese Sauce

Everyone has a spaghetti sauce recipe, a go-to sauce that you store in the freezer, thawing when you are feeling particularly uninspired about what to make for dinner. This Bolognese is my standard sauce recipe, one that I have returned to, tweaked a bit, and returned to again over the years. It's simmered for hours, and the result is thick, warming, and homey. The recipe doubles and even triples well, so freezing is always an option. The sauce that I made in occupational therapy at Vallejo wasn't quite this good, coming mostly from a can, but it was equally hearty.

2 tablespoons olive oil
1 onion, minced
1 carrot, minced
1 celery stalk, minced
½ cup diced prosciutto
½ pound ground beef
½ pound ground pork or
    veal

¾ cup dry white wine
28-ounce can whole
    tomatoes, drained
1 cup chicken stock
salt and pepper to taste
1 cup heavy cream, half-and-
    half, or milk

In a large deep skillet or dutch oven, heat the olive oil for 1 minute over medium heat. Add the onions, carrots, celery, and prosciutto and cook for about 10 minutes while stirring, until the vegetables are softened.

Add the ground meats and cook, breaking up any clumps, until no pink remains, about 5 minutes. Add the wine, turn the heat to medium-high, and cook until most of the liquid has evaporated, about 5 more minutes.

Crush the tomatoes with your hands, and then add them to the skillet along with the chicken stock. Bring to a boil, then turn the heat to low, and simmer, partially covered, stirring occasionally for 1 hour. After an hour has passed, taste, then season with salt and pepper. Simmer for an additional hour, or until most of the liquid has evaporated. The sauce should be very thick.

The sauce can be refrigerated for a few days at this point or frozen for several weeks. Reheat before completing the recipe.

Add the heavy cream, half-and-half, or milk and simmer for 15–30 minutes, stirring occasionally. Taste again for salt and pepper, then serve over your favorite pasta. I like fettuccine or tagliatelle.

makes approximately 1 quart

Meals on Wheels

Cruising down the long hospital corridors in my new mode of transportation, the wheelchair, I nodded to the other semi-lucid patients, each in their own wheeled thrones. Even if you could walk, the hospital had a wheelchair-only policy for liability reasons. During particularly busy afternoons, the hallway became a sea of bobbing wheelchairs. Trafficked by some unresponsive patient, it became a bottleneck of disabilities. Some patients did not adapt well to having to steer and push themselves around. They stopped in their tracks, waiting in the hallway for a nurse or unsuspecting orderly to take pity on them and push the chair to its next locale.

And there were quite a few locales, each marked with a different stripe down the hospital's corridor. The red stripe led to a vast gymnasium, unlike any gym I'd seen before. At one wall were tables of different heights; against another were stairs of random depths and heights, each with guardrails; and the centerpiece of the gymnasium was comprised of various sets of parallel bars. These were not the enormous parallel bars you see at the Olympic Games. No, the heights of these parallel bars were meant to brace us as we endeavored to slowly walk the length of the bars. They were learn-to-walk bars. The rest of the gym contained a small selection of free weights, various straps and large rubber bands called Therabands, and a few stationary bikes that remained covered in dust for my entire monthlong stay at Vallejo.

The green hallway stripe led to the occupational therapy room, the yellow to speech therapy, and the blue to various examination rooms. The tape was a veritable rainbow of all things therapeutic, but it served a specific purpose, and in those first days at Vallejo, when I was exhausted and bleary-eyed, I came to rely on those colored stripes of tape for direction, both in the obvious sense but also to make sense of what had happened and what was now expected of me. I simply needed to glance down at the laminated card on the armrest of my wheelchair to know where I was expected to be next. And I followed the red line from my room to the gymnasium after lunch, succumbing to the dictatorial rainbows.

I FOUND COMFORT in these colorful lines and in being a member of the rule-following contingent at Vallejo—but this was not always the case for me. When you are a child, it seems that you split into one of two groups: the followers or not necessarily the leaders but what I like to call the not-followers.

I hadn't always excelled at following directions or performing expected tasks. In another rainbow-themed building about eighteen years before, I had caused quite a ruckus. Preschool at

Montessori Children's House was held in a converted, rambling house with cement front steps that crookedly beckoned children inside. Each room of the house was set up with activities vaguely having to do with the room's original intent: the living room was the reading room, the kitchen was the "practical life" room, and so on. And the way my life has shaped up to be, it is no surprise that I loved the practical life room. Pouring beans from cup to cup was divine! Taking care of seedlings was fascinating! And watching roots burgeon out of a cut potato and into a water glass was endlessly amusing!

Mrs. Spare was the headmistress, and there was nothing spare about her. A large woman with gruff eyes and a mop of dyed brown hair, roots and temples staunchly gray, Mrs. Spare ruled over Montessori Children's House with an iron fist. It seemed that she had eyes in the back of her head, as she would call your name from across the house to reprimand you. She hated my fixation with the kitchen. She would constantly try to coax me out of that linoleum-covered room, but I would have no part of it. Ultimately, she called my mother in for a stern talk.

"Adrienne is not cooperating with how we run the house."

"Oh, how is that?" my mother replied, concern evident in her voice.

"Well, Mrs. Handler, no child leaves Montessori Children's House unprepared for the rigors of kindergarten. It is imperative that Adrienne learn how to read, as well as have familiarity with basic mathematics. And I cannot get her out of the practical life room of the house. I would like your help and assurance that you will go over these basic tenets with Adrienne at home."

"I'm sorry, Mrs. Spare," my mother replied. "It may be in the school's tradition to have their children racing toward 'the rigors of kindergarten,' as you say, but I really don't care if Adrienne knows how to read before she leaves Montessori. I believe in each child going at his or her own pace. Isn't that in fact one of the tenets of a Montessori education?"

And with that, my mother got up and left calmly, leaving Mrs. Spare gasping in a huff behind her.

So I guess you could say I was a not-follower early on. But here I was at Vallejo, expected to follow a very strict schedule. I didn't do it when I was three years old and had Mrs. Spare barking orders at me, but for my own well-being at age twenty-one, I succumbed to my physical therapist barking orders at me on a routine basis. I waited and I listened, taking every bit of advice from each therapist, expecting and wanting them to make me better. They had seen it all before, and I wanted to be the miracle girl, the girl who they spoke about to future patients as a symbol of hope. Each doctor and therapist commented on my age. "You have age on your side," they would say. As if my twenty-one years were my golden mean. And so for the first time in my life I listened exactly.

ALL OF THE physical therapists at Vallejo wore the requisite therapy uniform of navy blue trousers or track pants and a white polo shirt. I'm not really sure what accounted for the uniform; it was pretty clear who was who at the hospital. Crippled person, sagging on one side, maneuvering slowly in a wheelchair? Patient. Perky, endlessly cheerful person wearing blue pants? Physical therapist. The other telltale sign of a therapist? A foreign accent.

Cooking & Screaming

In my recollections of Vallejo, I favor histrionics, but despite the depressing dramatics, it was also a rather amazing place with a state-of-the-art gymnasium and a sea of physical therapists from around the world—but mostly Germany—all being trained to give you the best care possible. Patients were the therapists' test tubes, each filled with elixirs of promise or demise. Day in and day out, the therapists would stand before us, peering at the world through virginal Teutonic eyes, as a motley bunch of ragtag patients wheeled themselves into a somewhat orderly line and waited to be collected, begrudgingly ready for the day's activities to commence.

I have frequently imagined the foreign employee recruitment brochure for the program; in my mind, it read something like this:

Come to California for a summer filled with beautiful scenery as well as rewarding work. Work Monday through Friday in a state-of-the-art gymnasium and have your weekends free to explore EXCITING San Francisco as well as the GORGEOUS Napa Valley. Make lifelong friends and learn innovative approaches to physical therapy.

When it should have read:

Come to Vallejo. It's pretty far from San Francisco, and the wine country it isn't. Work harder than you ever have before with semilucid, unresponsive patients who will not have the slightest clue what you are telling them to do. Live in Strawberry Fields, the hospital-sanctioned condominiums across the street, enabling you to sleep in until the last possible minute, when your arduous day begins.

The truth is not always attractive.

I had lived my entire life in California, where the immigrant population abounds. As a child, my family hosted exchange students. I have extended family who are, in fact, German, so hearing accented English was nothing new for me. But this was not the case for other patients. Simple commands were met with "Huh?" And many patients did not respond to direction at all.

"Vee arf goin to voll offer, Mr. Smivf. Mr. Smivf . . . Mr. Smivf, voll offer."

Nothing.

A tap on the shoulder broke Mr. *Smith* from his reverie. A repeating of the command was met with a "What?" Frustrated by Mr. Smith's lack of response, the therapist got on the ground and rolled over slowly, showing Mr. Smith the exercise.

This happened routinely throughout the day. Not only was the physical exercise a frustration to the patient, but the manner in which it was taught was confounding to all involved.

Not all of the therapists were exports from other countries. There were a small number of "supertherapists" who had been working at Vallejo for years and were even allowed to strip off their uniforms once a week and sport track pants in the color of their choice. I met with my supertherapist at least once a day, sometimes twice, for one-on-one therapy sessions. These sessions were grueling. Not in the sweating-buckets-from-that-last-fifteen-minutes-on-the-elliptical-machine sense, but grueling in that it took all of my will to even raise my right leg up off the bed, let alone to raise this same leg to take one step forward. Physical therapy is a full-body, nonsexualized contact sport. It is very difficult to attempt to walk with a hulking therapist behind you, hands firmly planted on your hips, commanding, "Step, step, step. . . . Don't lead with your hips. Step. You're leading. Leave it. . . . Okay."

I had been a dancer; so standing at a barre was quite familiar to me. And the mirror, well that was just a necessary evil. I had spent the last ten years gazing at myself for hours a day. It was something that had always unnerved me, evaluating how I moved through space, the gentle curve of an extended arm and the raw muscularity of the leg, spotting myself during a pirouette or catching a glimpse of the air being sliced by my leg as I leapt into place. I preferred instead to feel, and I hoped that my body would intuitively know its proper placement. And it did, sometimes. But just as often, I would have dance teachers shrieking at me, their voices reverberating off the scratched Marley floors, "Look in the mirror, Adrienne! That's what it's there for!" So I would peer, though secretively and embarrassed. Staring in the mirror in public always seemed so narcissistic to me.

At Vallejo, staring in the mirror seemed to hold even greater consequences. Here I was not reprimanded by some Miss Havisham of a dance teacher; the therapists implored me to gaze in the mirror because I could no longer feel where my body was in space. It took such concentration to rise from my wheelchair and attempt to walk. I did not have an awareness of the right side of my body. The only way that I knew what the right side of my body was doing was to look at it directly—to watch it over and over again. I lifted my eyes upward and caught the reflection of the girl staring back at me in pink-striped pajama pants, with an elastic waistband for ease and no other closure. When I noticed her—my right arm poised not in arabesque but rather a crooked wing, elbow cocked, and wrist limp like a piece of pasta cooked way past al dente—the room began to spin, my knees grew weak, and I had to steady myself with my left hand on the walking bar to ensure that I remained upright.

EVERY DAY I followed the red line to the gymnasium, hoping that today was the day I would move with ease, breaking the confines of my disability. Hours were spent examining my walk using the parallel bars, or being manually stretched by a therapist, or trying to learn what it felt like to move smoothly once again. For all of my hours in the gymnasium, I spent a fraction of my time continually frustrated in the occupational therapy room—the therapy for your hands, fine motor skills, and upper body. I would follow the green line on the floor past the gym, my wheelchair waning to one side as I only had one arm and leg with which to navigate. The occupational therapy room looked very much like an elementary school classroom with a corrugated construction paper border tacked to the wall, a tumble of building blocks in the corner, and a kitchenette off to the side, arranged so that the patients could be in their very own "practical life" room. Once again, I was a child wearing pigtails, uninterested in the world outside of practical life. I wanted to spend all of my time in the kitchen, practicing something that was familiar to me. I was anxious to try to cut with my right hand grasping a dull knife. I wanted to try clutching the handle of an enamel saucepan, shiny material chipping off. I was eager to grip the teakettle and hoist it to waist height, to try the simple task of pouring. But this is not what happened. Instead, I was taught how to negotiate the kitchen one-armed.

When your brain suffers any sort of trauma—stroke, AVM, or otherwise—it swells. Just like any other part of the body. My brain was swollen. Once this swelling diminishes, therapists find that some patients can once again complete tasks that seemed impossible only weeks before. But as the weeks passed, the occupational therapists saw that there were still a considerable number of things I was unable to do: turning my right hand over was nearly impossible; opening my palm was inconceivable. Instead of waiting, opinions tarnished by what they had seen in the past with other patients, my occupational therapists taught me to become the one-armed chef rather than the one-and-a-fractioned-arm-chef.

In fact, I was taught to make an entire meal this way. There were some rather old men in my therapy group. It was a Saturday—group therapy day. Many of the therapists had the day off, so the rehabilitation hospital was forced to clump all of the patients together. These less than jolly gentlemen had grown tired of grunting "Huh?" to their physical therapists and were wheeled into the occupational therapy room.

In my group of three, there was the unresponsive man who sat slumped in his wheelchair, the responsive man who simply did not want to be there, and then there was me. My mother, who stayed with me continually, only leaving Vallejo when my sister would relieve her, wheeled me into the occupational therapy room. She took a seat, waiting to see what sort of mess would be made. We

35

were all wheeled into the kitchenette, where Sherise, the occupational therapist, excitedly proclaimed, "We're going to practice being in the kitchen today, so we're going to make this meal." She held up a laminated recipe card. Her proclamation was met with nothing from the unresponsive guy, a sarcastic "I can't wait" from the responsive guy, and a crooked smile from me.

The goal of occupational therapy is to practice what is important and worthwhile to the patient. As I glanced back and forth between my therapy mates, two men in their late sixties, it became clear that they had never cooked a meal in their lives. I could see this wouldn't quite be group therapy and more of my own experimentation in cooking. I would be making the meal that we all would enjoy.

I rose from my wheelchair slowly, using the arms of the seat to steady myself; I managed to lift my weighty limbs and limp the three steps to the counter. I leaned against the Formica, adjusting my eyes to read the laminated card. Spaghetti. That sounded easy enough. For the next hour, with Sherise's assistance, I made pasta sauce. The onion had been peeled for me and sliced in two to steady the process. I chopped with my left hand, my right hand placed gingerly on the countertop and bracing the onion. What weeks ago would have taken me seconds to complete, took me minutes, thinking of every motion that I had to make with the knife. I peeled garlic one-handed, fumbling with the papery shell. The pounds of blood-red ground meat I dumped into the pot landed with a thud, then a sizzle. Sherise opened four cans of generic tomato sauce for me, and one by one I poured them into an enormous stockpot. The sauce began to bubble as I sprinkled in a handful of Italian seasoning mix so old it was hardly fragrant.

Cooking & Screaming

Stirring left-handed, I did not want to leave the warmth of the kitchen. I felt good. And for a moment, I forgot about the life that I was living. Being in the kitchen—the sights and smells, the smear of crimson tomato sauce on my borrowed apron—felt a little bit like being at home. It didn't really matter that the sauce was only a slightly embellished red sauce from a can and not the traditional Bolognese with three kinds of meat and a mirepoix base that I had learned to make in college. I was still making it. The sauce percolated and the pasta boiled. We sat and enjoyed the sauce of my labors, heaped on piles of slithery spaghetti noodles. I ate. And ate. Two huge bowls. After I had heartily consumed the second bowl and was readying for another, my mother stopped me, seeing my belly expand beneath my elastic-waisted pants. I didn't feel full. After weeks of IVs and pizza casseroles, I had forgotten what it felt like to be hungry or to be satiated. It felt good to be eating. With each slurp of limp spaghetti coated in far too much shirt-staining sauce, I was replenishing what these past weeks had taken from me—my independence, my headstrong nature, my happiness. Who knows if I ever would have stopped eating?

CHAPTER 4

Chili à la Wendy

Chili recipes are to American cooking as soufflé recipes are to French cooking; many people claim to have an unbeatable one. When I was growing up, I knew a woman with a secret chili recipe, which she stewed and simmered on the stove for three days. Three. Days. It was good chili—don't get me wrong—but I don't really have the dedication to make that, even if she were to give me the recipe. In Vallejo, chili was one of my first foods from the outside world. That chili wasn't simmered for days—it wasn't even homemade—but it did the trick. My chili recipe is in homage to that chili. Simmered and on the table in hours rather than days, it develops a richer flavor by sitting in the fridge for a day or so. Like many Cincinnati chilis, this uses a bit of unsweetened cocoa powder. I find the cocoa adds a savory depth to this meal. Cornbread goes great with this dish.

2 tablespoons olive oil
2 small onions or 1 large
   onion, diced
3 cloves garlic, sliced
1½ pounds ground beef
3 tablespoons chili powder
1 tablespoon unsweetened
   cocoa powder
1½ teaspoons ground cumin
1 tablespoon all-purpose
   flour

28-ounce can tomato puree
   (not sauce) or diced
   tomatoes with juice
1 cup water
15-ounce can kidney beans,
   rinsed and drained
salt to taste
Cheddar cheese (optional)
Scallions (optional)

In a dutch oven or deep skillet, heat the olive oil on medium-high. Add the onions, garlic, and ground beef. Cook until the meat is thoroughly browned. Drain the fat from the pan if desired.

Add the chili powder, cocoa powder, cumin, and flour and cook for 2–3 minutes over high heat. Add the tomato puree or diced tomatoes and the water and bring to a boil. Continue boiling for 5 minutes, then reduce the heat to a simmer and cook for 45 minutes, partially covered, stirring occasionally.

Add the kidney beans and cook for 5 minutes, until the beans are heated through. Season with a healthy dose of salt. You may want to garnish with grated sharp Cheddar cheese and chopped scallions.

serves 4–6

Comfort Food

So, Adrienne, you have had quite a life-altering experience?"

Was that even a question? It seemed more like a fact to me. But phrased in such a way, closing the sentence with the rising intonation of Dr. Lomanico's nasal voice, I knew that I was expected to respond. We were going to play the rhetorical question game.

"Yes," I mumbled. This was my first experience with psychotherapy, and it was not at all what I anticipated it to be. It's not that I never thought about psychotherapy. In fact, I could imagine going to see a shrink later in life, when the perils of day-to-day life might seem too extreme for me to confront on my own. I would walk into a modern office and a properly dressed older woman with salt-and-pepper hair, crimson lips, and onyx glasses too large for her face would greet me. She would sit behind a teak desk and I would take my place on the worn leather of a Le Corbusier lounge. And then I would begin expelling the entire minutia of my neurotic life.

But Dr. Lomanico, with his pockmarked skin, vomit-like Impressionistic ties, and shit-eating grin, was hardly the therapist of my dreams. We had no connection, and I could tell, as he glanced at his watch for the umpteenth time during our session, he was waiting to hop in his new Mercedes and speed off to the Napa Valley, racing home to his wife and two small children. And who could blame him? It wasn't like I wanted to be there either, but he was my assigned neuropsychologist, the only neuropsychologist available at Vallejo, and a healthy mind is a healthy body. Or at least that's what Dr. Lomanico would tell me on a consistent basis.

Vallejo had become a struggle for me. In a sense, I treated rehabilitation like it was summer school—a difficult place to be when there were swimming pools to jump into and barbecues to attend. It was hard for me to believe that only two months ago I had been a college student, trudging back to my apartment with a satchel full of classic novels, handouts, and a sweaty, crumpled mass of dance clothes in need of washing. I had always split my time between dance and schoolwork, practice and lectures, but here at Vallejo, my time was split between rehabilitation and memories of what once was.

I was nearing the end of my stay at the rehabilitation hospital. Of course, I had thoughts welling up inside me, fears about the future, and a longing to get back to the life that had been taken from me. I certainly needed help, but continuously being asked the perennial question, "How do you feel?" from a doctor with whom I felt no connection was not the help that I needed.

"So what's on the agenda for when you get back?" Dr. Lomanico questioned. I stared at him blankly, catatonic. Did I really feel like answering him truthfully? I hadn't a clue what the future held, and I was terrified.

The pit in the bottom of my stomach was similar to the one I would get each summer when I got ready to go to sleepaway camp. I was scared of the unknown. Who would my counselors be? Would I like my bunkmates? I would tell my mom over and over as she packed my suitcase—shorts on one side, T-shirts on the other, separated by a row of neatly folded underwear—that I was terrified. Absolutely, under no circumstances, did I want to leave the family. My mother would nod her head, "I know, you say this every year, and every year you love camp. We hear about it for the rest of the summer."

"But this year is different," I would plead. "This year I *really* don't want to go." As I got in the car, ready to make the two-hour trip away from home to Camp Swig in the Santa Cruz Mountains, the bellyache of homesickness was omnipresent. But my stomach maladies would retreat in a day's time, as soon as I met my counselors and saw the lush redwood groves, the hiking trails leading to sparkling fields of wildflowers, and the familiar faces of fellow campers. The pleading would become a distant memory as I became consumed with lanyards and campfires.

Here I was, over a decade later, sitting in a creaky chair in Dr. Lomanico's sterile office, feeling that same trepidation. The words were there; I just wasn't able to succinctly formulate the quip that I wanted. Speaking was a trial. There was so much that I wanted to express: I wanted to say that I was terrified of the future, that I was worried about my recovery, that I was irritated with the doctors for never really telling me what I could expect to achieve, that I was angry for being dealt such a devastating blow, that I was saddened for my parents, that at times I felt the only thing left to do was open my mouth and let out a bloodcurdling scream. But I couldn't pluck the words from space. So instead I calmly said, "You know, I'm not really sure. More therapy I suppose. . . . Fun." Fun, there, at least I was able to muster up a bit of sarcasm for him. I smirked.

"Well, Adrienne, I'm glad you see your therapy as fun," Dr. Lomanico said without the slightest hint of irony. "It certainly is beneficial. If you can manage to see the intrigue in something you have to do, all the better." I was dumbfounded at his remark. Had he ever heard sarcasm before? What more could I do? I went along with the rest of my "therapy" session.

At the end of my Vallejo stay, Dr. Lomanico had to produce a brief write-up about my sessions with him and what sort of mental state he thought I was in. It read:

> Patient is in stable condition. Adrienne seems to realize the magnitude of her situation, but is more than willing to work, becoming a functioning member of society once again. Her positive attitude was inspiring. For such a young person, she seems bright and eager to work, even in the face of adversity.

Putz.

IT WAS 8:30 in the evening, I was lying in bed. My television had been flipped on by a nurse performing the nightly ritual of serving dinner and then readying her patients for bed. I stared at a PBS reality show about modern-day families going back to frontier times and forging a life for themselves. The whole *Little House on the Prairie* thing wasn't really working for me, especially because one of the modern-day Laura Ingalls Wilders was wearing gobs of mascara, and apparently not the waterproof sort, as it was smudged underneath her eyes making her look like a raccoon. My sister briskly walked into the room. Jennifer had been staying with me at the hospital for a few days.

My sister and I had always been close. As we grew up, our age difference seemed inconsequential. With adulthood came a new bond; Jennifer was my best friend. There was Maia, and there was my boyfriend, Brian, people who I loved dearly. But there is something about knowing a person from the beginning. Sharing in your joys, knowing your foibles, and—you can't ignore—lamenting with you about your parents.

"Hey A, whatcha doin'?"

I shrugged. "What did you get yourself for dinner?" Any bit of conversation was more interesting than this reality show.

"Well, it looks like tonight's treat is Wendy's."

Vallejo was a culinary wasteland. The only restaurants surrounding the rehabilitation hospital were fast-food establishments. A bastion of progressive health surrounded by vats of oil and deep-fat fryers. She pulled out a cup of chili and a soggy baked potato from her Wendy's bag, crinkling the image of the befreckled little girl with bright red hair.

"Do you want some?"

I thought of the grilled chicken breast I had choked down for dinner a few hours before, the grill marks no doubt painted on in some processing plant. The floppy steamed broccoli and the bright lime Jell-O cup had hardly been satisfying. Since Donna had brought me the pizza casserole weeks before, I had been eating unappetizing assemblages of food. "Sure," I said. Jennifer took the lid off the chili and pulled the rolling table toward the bed. I took my first bite of chili, warm but not hot. It was soupy and burnt red in color, with chunks of soggy peppers and glossy onions drowning in tomato sauce. I dunked the spoon in again. This time the utensil emerged with small clumps of ground meat. This was chili con carne. Then I took another bite. And yet another.

"Mmm . . . this is like—the best chili I have ever eaten." I'm not sure what it was about the chili, but to me, on that day, it *was* the best chili ever. Maybe it was that I was finally eating what everyone else in the world could eat, not hermetically sealed astronaut food, or maybe it was that the chili actually had flavor, albeit salt. But that night, let's just say Jennifer had a splendid dinner at the vending machine while I ravenously consumed her Wendy's chili.

"ARE YOU READY?" my mom asked pleasantly as I gazed out my hospital room window toward the sea of cars parked around the building. I nodded, because I *was* ready. My bags were packed. Piles of new T-shirts bought from a discount store and stacks of elasticized pajama bottoms, which had become my uniform, were all neatly packed away by my mother as she had done years before—tops on one side of the suitcase, bottoms on the other, and separated by a row of underwear. There were bundles of cards, from everyone I had ever met, and bouquets of flowers, the gladiolas now beginning to brown and wilt after weeks of breathing stale enclosed air. But everything came with me, even the wilted flowers, acting as not-so-subtle reminders of where I had been.

I scootched, bracing myself with my left hand, from the bed into my wheelchair, and bending down, I released the hand brake. I wheeled myself into the hallway, stopping at the nurses' station to say good-bye. For the past few weeks, they had acted like my parents when my parents were unable to be there. They brought me my meals, changed my bedding, and, even though the air outside was hot and dry, brought me extra blankets to cut the chilly air-conditioned draft. I hugged the nurses and thanked them for all they had done. My actions were met with a bevy of, "Don't worry, hon. You'll do great!" and, "You'll be back dancing in no time!" and, "We'll see you soon, walking around, for checkup!" And I wanted to believe them, but I was scared.

Each doctor who I spoke with at Vallejo and those I spoke with subsequently were far less committal when met with the question: "How much movement can I expect to get back?" I imagine that doctors sit in some giant lecture hall at medical school learning how to be purposely evasive when it comes to answering difficult questions. It's as if the Hippocratic oath has a clause regarding what to tell expectant patients: nothing. I understand why to some extent. Each patient is different, some people's injuries are greater than others, and some want it more—they have that undying urge to get well again. But I wanted it badly and was willing to try anything.

Stopping by the gym, I said good-bye to my physical therapists. Each had a reminder for me: "Remember not to throw your hips forward with each step." I nodded. "If nothing else, weight-bear." Of course. "Just relax." I would try. Would all of these things make me feel—and appear—more normal? Here I thought that

I was finished with school, but now it seemed that not only did I have hours of homework, but it was of dire consequence. How could I be expected to "just relax" when each movement that I made was calculated?

I had never really been a self-conscious person. In high school, I dyed my hair purple, often wore a hideous crocheted vest of my aunt's from the seventies, donned a tutu to the prom, and wore too much eye makeup. I did what I wanted, whether I stood out in a crowd or disappeared into the recesses. But Vallejo had changed me. There I had become self-conscious, and not in the lipstick-on-your-teeth sort of way. I was hyperaware of my surroundings and how I was being perceived by others. I hung onto every person's word. When I was told to "just relax," what did that mean? In dance there is a term called muscle memory, where your body subconsciously takes over the movement. The actions become not so much about the lines of choreography but rather an automatic flow learned through repetition. Is *that* what was expected of me? Or when I was told to "just relax," was it on an emotional level? Did a therapist want me not to fret over how I was moving? It all seemed so complicated. I had been allowing someone else—a doctor, a therapist, a nurse, my parents—to take the reigns and guide me. In a sense, I didn't want the responsibility of making those decisions. It was much easier to sit back and let others speak of me as an apparition of myself. By making decisions about my health and my future, I was admitting that this was my life now, but this was not the life that I had picked.

My mother wheeled me out to the car, packed all of my bags into the trunk, and loaded me into the passenger seat. My wheelchair, folded like an intricate puzzle, was placed in the backseat. "Okay . . . let's go," she said, resting her hand on my knee. As we drove away, I stared forward, watching the hospital building in the side mirror grow smaller and smaller. I craned my head to catch a final glimpse of the concrete monolith that I called home for the last month. It felt like a cocoon from the inside, completely disorienting. And as my mom drove on, the world looked different to me.

I peered out the window, laying my head back on the seat, and stared at the highway. I hadn't seen anything besides the four walls of the hospital for such a long time that even the slick gray pavement of the freeway was astoundingly beautiful. I had been holed up in disinfectant-scented rooms; my peers had been invalids; I had forgotten about the whole world beyond the confines of the rehabilitation hospital. That world now existed for me as well. We hit traffic coming down I-80. There was the same mysterious bottleneck as always, where the highway turns from suburban thoroughfare to urban highway. It was July in the Bay Area and summer had finally come. The car crawled onward, and the flats of the bay glistened a bluish gray against the rolling hills of the Berkeley Marina. But we weren't stopping. We continued driving, past the university, past the Craftsman bungalows and the amazing cheese shop that helped me confront my cheese taboo, past my apartment above the bakery that sold granola chocolate-chip cookies, pizza bread, and Danish filled with tart apricot compote.

We were going home. To the place where I had grown up. Where my parents still lived and worked—but a place that I had not called *my* home for four years. It didn't matter to me that my dance clothes were, no doubt, left in a heap on my bedroom floor in Berkeley; the novel I had been cramming to finish for finals was left open; the bowl with remains of tagliatelle with zucchini was probably growing mold in the sink. I was happy to be out of Vallejo, but I knew that all of my work would soon continue, across the bay, at my parents' home.

CHAPTER 5

Fish en Papillote, Provençal Style

Fish en papillote. The name alone sounds intimidating, but this dish is so simple that even a college student living on her own for the first time can make it for her new boyfriend. At least that's what I did. Translated, en papillote means "cooked in parchment paper." The fish and vegetables steam in their own juice, which is rendered from the baking process—very pleasing and very healthy. The dish is superb and looks impressive when brought to the table. It is delicious and easy to make, which is appealing after a weekend of carousing or ingesting a lot of rich foods. So go out, party, eat a bunch of foie gras, sleep very little, then come home and treat yourself to a papillote.

olive oil for drizzling

1 medium-size waxy potato, very thinly sliced

salt and pepper to taste

½ pound white fish fillet (like cod, red snapper, tilapia, etc.) divided into two portions

1 cup green beans, cut into bite-size pieces

2 cups chopped mushrooms (crimini, shiitake, oyster, etc.)

15 olives (niçoise, oil cured, kalamata, etc.)

2 sprigs fresh thyme

1 tablespoon unsalted butter

Preheat the oven to 425°F. Begin by cutting two large circles in parchment paper. You could use aluminum foil in a pinch.

Fold each circle in half; the radius should be 6–8 inches. Open each circle and place on a baking sheet.

You will only be putting ingredients on half of each circle. Drizzle olive oil on the bottom of each half circle and spread the potatoes, evenly divided, on top of the oil. Drizzle a bit more olive oil, then season with salt and pepper. Place the fish fillet on top, rub a little olive oil on each fillet, and season again with salt and pepper. Sprinkle the green beans, mushrooms, and olives on each fillet. Finish off each packet with a sprig of thyme and ½ tablespoon of butter.

Now take the free half of parchment and place it over the fillet. Close each packet by crimping and rolling the parchment. The idea is to create a neat, steaming vessel for the fillet. Once each packet is complete, place the baking sheet in the oven for 20 minutes. Transfer each packet to a plate. Carefully cut open the parchment and dig in.

serves 2

Fish on Fridays

Many **of the important** conversations in my life, for one reason or another, have taken place in the car. I had the sex talk with my mom while driving home from a day of running errands in our old gargantuan LTD Crown Victoria. I was five, and my grandma watched soap operas; therefore, I, too, watched soap operas during my afternoons at her house. After seeing too many couples getting busy on TV, or watching Marlena and Roman discuss their "lovemaking" in a passionate debate on *Days of Our Lives*, I had to know what the big deal was. So my mother told me only what I needed to know while gripping the steering wheel, her knuckles white. In high school, I had a friend who picked me up in her rusty pickup truck and regaled me with personal details of how she had lost her virginity. I never asked her where this had taken place, thinking that she probably lost it on the same seat of her old pickup. And one month after my return home from Vallejo, I tried to break up with Brian, my boyfriend, while he was driving us home from breakfast.

"I want you to know that if this is too much for you, I understand," I said as casually as possible, though this was something I had been thinking about for quite some time. I had talked about it with my sister. She listened closely, telling me not to make any rash decisions and that I had gone through enough changes in my life. She thought the best thing to do was talk it over with Brian. So I waited until the next morning that we spent together.

"What?" he asked. But not in a frantic, how-could-you-do-this sort of way, but rather in a could-you-repeat-that-I'm-driving-therefore-not-really-paying-attention sort of way.

"I'm just saying that right now everything is sort of crazy." I gestured to the limp right side of my body and folded-up wheelchair in the backseat of his beat-up Toyota. "I would understand. I mean, in fact, it might even be better for me. I could just focus on therapy." I said all of these things, not even sure if they were exactly what I meant. Words swirled around in my head, and I attempted to pluck them out of my consciousness and formulate a complete sentence. These days, I always seemed to be in a fog.

"Wait—what are you saying?" Brian asked, making a right-hand turn onto my parents' street.

"It's just hard. It will be hard."

"And you think I don't know this? I've seen you work; I know the effort you put into it all."

Brian had been one of the few people who I allowed to see me in Vallejo. The rest of the world seemed like a distraction. I was embarrassed that I needed assistance to tie my shoes or even to unscrew the cap on the toothpaste tube. But I let Brian into my new world of disability. Maybe it was because Maia called Brian after calling my parents that dark May day, and together they waited under the harsh lights of the hospital for my mother and sister to arrive, or maybe it was because I knew that the people who love you will never judge you.

But now that I was home, things were even more manic than they had been at Vallejo. There everything had been consolidated into one therapeutic place; I breathed, slept, and ate therapy. Things were different at my parents' house. The real world was involved. People bustled around me, made dates for lunch with friends, stopped to pick up dry cleaning on their way home from work, prepared dinner, then zoned out in front of the television set. And there I sat in my wheelchair as life went rapidly on. I always seemed to have an appointment to go to. Doctors' offices, several physical therapy sessions per week, fruitless occupational therapy sessions, meetings with a speech therapist who was obsessed with my recent graduation from UC Berkeley—although being in a coma had made it impossible for me to put on the cap and gown. Then there was homework, but not like the assignments and theses at college. These assignments were daily and repetitive, lacking deadlines. My bedroom at my parents' house had become an ersatz gym for weaklings. There were Therabands as well as Theratubes (the stiffer, tube-like sister of the Theraband) and photocopied handouts detailing stretches for various parts of the body from my pack of physical therapists. There were blocks to try to grasp, braces for my right leg, and contraptions for my right arm. Exercises were expected to be performed several times a day. It seemed that I barely had enough time to put away the

Theraband before the Theratube was called upon for another purpose . . . like wringing my own neck. And I was always tired. I wanted to scream, demand that the world stop for just a moment.

On the weekends, Brian came down from Berkeley to see me. I wasn't sure if I was becoming more of a nuisance than a helpful diversion from his academic life. He would come to sleep over at my parents' house, with me in my high school bed, in my childhood room. I had never thought that my parents were the type to look the other way and let my boyfriend spend the night with me. But I guess allowances are made in extreme circumstances. Sometimes we would go out for breakfast, a usual activity for the two of us in Berkeley. I tried to be nonchalant and happy, sitting in front of my french toast, my right hand still sleeping in my lap. But then I would think of my wheelchair, folded up in the trunk of Brian's car, in case we decided to travel somewhere that required a walk, and my face would become flushed with anger.

Driving home that morning, I wasn't sure what I truly wanted, but I knew that these feelings somehow needed to be expressed. "It's okay. We'll take it all as it comes. Don't worry about us . . . you have enough to worry about," he said gently.

I didn't say anything. Partly because the whole subject exhausted me. The thought of doing anything more—making any more huge changes in my life—seemed ridiculous. But partly because I knew Brian was right. He had been my boyfriend for a little over a year, pre-AVM. I wanted him to stay for the right reasons and to know that I understood if for some reason he couldn't.

But he stuck around for good. And he gained a wife out of the deal.

Cooking & Screaming

. . .

IN COLLEGE, I was hardly beating the boys off with sticks. Maybe it was because I always had that proverbial stick poised and ready to strike at the slightest bit of irritation, but I guess I will never truly know. Evenings were spent with Maia, drinking tea, watching indie movies on video, lamenting our fate—misery loves company—and remarking about how lame all of the boys our age were. And then I met Brian.

I actually picked him up at a cafe that Maia and I frequented. When we first met, Brian had graduated from UC Berkeley and was making his living as a jazz musician. He looked like Elvis Costello, the early years. Black hair, black framed glasses, and skinny as all get out. Exactly my type. I had seen him perform a few times in San Francisco, hunched over his electric guitar, cradling it like a musical baby. So imagine my surprise when he stood in front of me on line one day, ordering a latté. We smiled in recognition. He was reading Proust, I, Walpole, and Maia and I offered him a chair at our table at Mocha Lisa.

The first meal that I made for him, two weeks into our relationship, was an Asian take on fish en papillote—which is only an intimidating way of saying fish baked in parchment paper. I was obsessed with enoki mushrooms—those straw-colored, spindly fungi that grow in clumps and taste like practically nothing, yet have the chewy texture of a Japanese soba noodle. A bit of salmon, some snow peas, a handful of baby bok choy, and my darling little fungi all went into parchment paper envelopes with a healthy dose of hoisin sauce and a sprinkling of toasted sesame oil. Twenty minutes later, precisely the time it took to steam some rice, and the fish was done. And Brian ate it all up. In fact, not only did he eat his portion, he ate my leftovers as well, even though I had eaten all of the enokis.

"And that was so easy. I'll have to remember how to do that at home." But he didn't. In fact, he rarely does any of the cooking at home, which works out fine, because he is an excellent dishwasher. In addition to being a great domestic help, he is also the smartest, kindest, funniest, most understanding person I have ever met. He talks about both Husserlian phenomenology and the latest episode of *Project Runway* with conviction.

Brian has a quick wit and a sharp tongue, but he is also an astute listener. When I am flummoxed, he is calming; when he is esoteric, I am grounded.

It is as if my life has been split into two stories—pre-AVM and post-AVM—and Brian straddles both. My pre-AVM life is like a piece of theater, playing over in my mind. A swelling soundtrack of strings, a rosy glow, and characters dancing in and out of each frame, always on two feet, never limping, with both arms outstretched before them. Then there is the post-AVM life, often fraught with anxieties and self-imposed rules, doctors and therapists of all sorts. This image is fragile, though it still holds a certain power over me. It can strangle me. And Brian knows each side of me. He is the person I go to when I begin to feel sorry for myself, when life seems a bit too hard, when I begin to miss my old life. He is also the person I go to to celebrate the triumphs and to share laughs. And he has a voracious appetite for my cooking. What more could a girl ask for?

CHAPTER 6

Julienned Brussels Sprouts

If you are a Brussels sprout novice or think that you don't like this little cabbage-shaped vegetable, this is the recipe to try. Once julienned, brussels sprouts lose their somewhat bitter flavor and become a delightful side dish. To julienne the sprouts, I use a mandoline, but it can be done with a knife instead. To me, Brussels sprouts mean Thanksgiving. They are festive and relatively easy to prepare, and they happened to be my contribution to the Thanksgiving meal when I was out of the hospital.

4 shallots, thinly sliced
2 tablespoons olive oil
salt and pepper to taste
5 cups julienned Brussels
sprouts (16–20 whole
sprouts)
½ cup heavy cream or half-
and-half

In a large skillet, over medium heat, brown the shallots in the olive oil and season with salt and pepper. Once the shallots get a bit of color, add the julienned sprouts, mixing well to evenly disperse the shallots. Brown the Brussels sprouts slightly. Add the heavy cream or half-and-half and a bit more salt and pepper, cover the skillet, and turn the heat to medium-low to steam the Brussels sprouts. When the skillet is just about dry, 5–7 minutes, taste for doneness and seasoning. The Brussels sprouts should be crisp-tender and buttery tasting due to the cream.

serves 4–6

On the Side

When **I was young** and couldn't fall asleep, my mother taught me a little game that always made her tired, when she couldn't sleep.

"Lie still on your back," she told me. "Close your eyes and breathe in deeply. Now tense up your toes, hold them tight for five seconds, then release. Next, your lower legs and your toes. Hold them . . . hold them . . . all right, let go." Eventually, I would do this with my entire body, incrementally. I wasn't sure if it was actually the exercise, or maybe it was the concentration, but by the end, my body would lay limp and I would drift off peacefully.

Now, the right side of my body was always tense. I longed for the moment of eventual release, but it would not come. It was as if I had the toned body of an athlete; you could bounce nickels off the tension in my leg. No matter how much I concentrated on relaxation or thought about my listless body in space, I could not relax. So, instead, I thought about motion. And rather than focusing on the minutia of moving my digits, which at this time seemed like a Herculean feat, I focused on grand movements. Not moving my fingers but rather moving my entire arm upward and off the bed. I would tell myself not to worry about my wrist; it was more important to raise my entire arm above my head. At night, after the lights were out and I still couldn't sleep, my mind racing with all of the day's activities, I would try to move.

My arm felt so heavy. It was as if a giant was placing his hand on it, begging and taunting me to wrestle my extremity free. But one night, as I lay restless in bed, I managed, ever so slightly, to wrangle my arm and get it to move. It was levitating, maybe four inches above my prone abdomen. I held it and held it for what seemed like eternity but was really only seconds. And then it came crashing down beside me. I beamed in the darkness. After moments of rest, I attempted the impossible again. This time, I was able to hold my arm one foot from the bed before it came careening down. I was ecstatic. My brain was actually sending messages to my body—the correct messages—and my body was responding. I was moving with intention.

I stayed in bed, hesitant to move too much or I might jinx my good fortune. But after several more successful attempts, I called out for my mother. A late-night call, even one from the bedroom down the hall, was the last thing she wanted to hear. My dad had his stroke in the middle of the night and my grandma passed away after the eleven o'clock news, so my mother did not want to hear the voice of her daughter echoing from down the hall. She got up out of bed, scrambled down the hallway, and flipped on the light in my room. She found me, not fallen limp in distress but lying in bed, the sheet jumbled up beside me, with my right arm stretched out above me, wrist dangling and hand limp. My arm was waving upward at a ninety-degree angle from my prostrate body. It took her a moment to calm down and take it all in, but once she did, a smile slowly took shape on her face. And once again my arm came crashing down.

MY DAYS WERE long and repetitious, occasionally punctuated by a friend from my past. I saw Brian each week, either during the week in between his gigs or on the weekends. He was enjoying being back in school and getting lost in the world of academic composing. Maia would come on the weekends. She had a new boyfriend, Gabe, whom she ecstatically told me all about. And then there was our mutual friend David.

David and Maia had lived in the dorms together freshman year, commiserating over snotty roommates, wretched food, and the loss of all personal privacies. When I met Maia, I met David as well. He was clever, with a mocking tone and a sarcastic streak; he was not an easy person to befriend. But once you did, you had a friend for life. David was the type of person who would bring you soup when you were sick, along with the newest punk album he was into, to rock out to during your recuperation.

David was cute, in a Hardy Boys sort of way, a description I think that he was all too familiar with and fought against in a decisive way. His hair was always cropped short, very clean-cut, but the color seemed to change on an almost weekly basis according to his whim—green one week, pink the next, rainbow the week following—it was his trademark. David was from Massachusetts, a rarity of sorts to be attending school in the University of California system, but he had a reason. The winters in Massachusetts proved too difficult for a person in a wheelchair. Icy snowdrifts are difficult for a four-wheel-drive truck to plow through; imagine what it is like for a boy-powered, two-wheel-drive, manual wheelchair. So California it was, where the most you ever have to contend with is a rainy day. And although David would never acknowledge it, Berkeley is a very wheelchair-friendly city.

In college, Maia introduced me to David over a rousing game of Scrabble. On the way home, I asked Maia about his past. "Has he always been in a wheelchair?"

"You know, I don't even know."

I, ever the intrusive conversationalist, was shocked. "You mean you never asked him?"

"No, I never asked him. And he never talks about it. Maybe he wants to keep it to himself."

I thought carefully about this. Of course, David had the right to keep this information private, but how could he? "But isn't it like the elephant in the room? How can his wheelchair not be addressed?"

"It just isn't. David and I have been friends for a while. I feel like my window of opportunity has passed. If I really wanted to know, I feel like I would have had to ask about it sooner in our relationship."

"I understand that. But doesn't not knowing drive you crazy?"

"I guess it doesn't."

"My god, he's not even *my* friend and it drives me insane."

"Well, I guess I'm just a bigger person than you," Maia said with a laugh.

"I guess so."

Cooking & Screaming

The more I hung out with Maia and David, the less important knowing the details of David and his wheelchair became. Call it my immaturity, but I wore my friendship with David as a badge for disability rights. Not that he asked me to; in fact, I think that he would have killed me if he knew. But it was college. For the first time in my life, I was making decisions on my own, and I had decided to have a friend with a disability. Petty—yes, understandable—completely. At home, I had never known someone with a disability. In middle school, I would see students from the special education class rolling around in large motorized wheelchairs. They had a special table in the cafeteria, a group of disabled children and their caregivers.

At Berkeley, however, differences became the norm. People are living on their own for the first time in their young lives. Hair gets longer for boys, shorter for girls, and new friends come from different socioeconomic backgrounds, creeds, and races. I had a friend who was in a wheelchair, and it made no difference at all.

David was uncharacteristically understanding when he found out about my AVM. The usual sarcasm was nonexistent; David must have known that my ego was too fragile to handle his comments. I half expected him to tease me about my limp—that's how the David I had known would have acted. But there were no jokes and no teasing. When I was released from the hospital and recuperating at my parents' house, David drove across the bay to see me one afternoon. I hadn't seen much of anyone. I was waiting for that moment when I would be healed to suddenly appear one day. People would be shocked and complimentary. "Therapy was a bitch," I would say. "But look at me now. I couldn't wait for it to be over." So I kept myself cloistered from many, waiting to be "normal" again. When David suggested that he come over for a visit, I obliged. With David I could talk, or better yet, not talk, about what had physically transpired for me. I thought that I needed someone who had been there himself to tell me how to navigate the world. It was all so new to me, but it was not for David.

The morning of David's visit, I tried to brush up on my Scrabble words in the dictionary, but I hoped that it wouldn't be necessary—what I really wanted to do was talk, not play board games. When I heard David's car pull up in the driveway, I rose from the foot of my bed, gathered my sweater and my gleaming four-prong cane, and made my way to the front door. I would meet him outside, so he wouldn't have to get out of the car.

Watching David fold up his wheelchair, disassemble the wheels, and place them each on the floor behind the driver's seat was like watching a magician take a rabbit out of a hat. He would push himself up and out of the chair and into the car, and then the sleight of hand would begin. He would keep the conversation going, knowing full well that his passengers were in secret awe. It was as if he had memorized the hooks and latches of the chair and could take it apart with his eyes closed.

Making my way toward David's car, I left my cane to stand like a totem pole near the car door, and with my one good hand, opened it.

"Long time no see," remarked David.

"I know. It's been a while." I scanned David's face for some sign of judgment, but he played it cool.

"So, where to?"

"I don't know. Maybe we could go and get a cup of coffee.

There's a place nearby that has board games. I'm sure they have Scrabble."

"Aha," said David, wringing his hands. "If you're up for an ass-whooping, I'm definitely good for it. Show me the way."

We wound our way through the hills, passing each home with its well-manicured lawn. When we arrived at the coffee shop, there was a parallel parking spot right in front. I crawled out of the car awkwardly and waited for David to reassemble his wheelchair, careful to avert my eyes while he leveraged himself from one wheeled mode of transportation to another. I always snuck glances at David's feats. I imagined that a person who never talked about his disability did not want to be made a spectacle. Then we made our way into the coffee shop, the hobbling girl and the wheelchaired boy. My cane became another appendage, a stiff third leg that jutted out in front of me, and David's wheelchair was like a shining beacon of our collective disability. In the coffee shop, people stepped aside for us, politely yet condescendingly. We ordered our drinks, and the barista didn't call out our names to pick up our coffees. Instead, he said, "Don't worry about it. I'll bring the coffees to you." It was a friendly sentiment—and one that David and I actually needed—but I resented his generosity. Hanging out with David no longer made me proud of having a friend who had a disability; it made me self-conscious of my own disability.

We played Scrabble. That is all that we did. David did not ask about my health or my therapy, and I kept pretending that he was not in a wheelchair. Our respective elephants in the room had pitched a tent, lit a raging bonfire, and were warming their trunks in front of it. I had expected an open conversation from

David. His demeanor had been so calm, so reassuring over the telephone; I wanted that same person to appear to me over coffee and Scrabble. Instead, the silence was deafening, and I felt like an immature adolescent—if he wasn't going to talk, well, I wasn't going to either. Aligning myself with David and following his lead, never speaking of what was happening to me, was a huge act of denial.

How could David and I not address disability while every able-bodied person around us noticed it so openly? We now had truly unique experiences in common, but neither one of us was evolved enough to discuss it. There was this conflicted ambivalence that became evident in our relationship. Perhaps David was so evolved that he did not need to address it, but yet, as he made his way toward the exit after our stellar game of Scrabble, making jokes about my pitiful six-point words, I doubted that was the case. It seemed I would have to look for resolution elsewhere.

David and I spoke on the phone a few more times that year. He had stayed in Berkeley after graduation and would mention the obscure punk bands or the latest graffiti artist whose work was on display in Oakland. But as time passed, our telephone calls grew more infrequent as I struggled to make my relationship with David into something it was not. Yes, we were both disabled, but I needed to find what that meant to me. David would not be my model.

HOSPITAL GOWNS HAD become my new second wardrobe, and I had grown accustomed to the shocking chill of a stethoscope way back in June. There were appointments too numerous to count, making me busier than I had been in those final days of college.

In my brief moments of downtime, I would often pick up a novel, but it was difficult to focus. I would flip on the television, but my mind would wander. So, I would stumble into the kitchen.

It is funny how two children coming from the same family can have such different likes and dislikes. I had always been fascinated by the clanging of pots and the warmth of the stove. While growing up, my mother would stand in the kitchen with her two girls beside her, baking a batch of cookies on a Sunday afternoon. Jennifer would pour in the fragrant vanilla extract; I would measure out the cups of flour, letting the particles fall like snow around us; and my mom would do the mixing. But my sister would leave the kitchen as soon as the batter was complete. I stayed by the oven, smelling the baking sugar and waiting until the buzzer chimed and the cookies were complete. I took great satisfaction in finishing my cookie-making project. Of course, I wanted to taste the sweet, crisp final product, but I appreciated the entire process.

I guess it is no surprise that my fixation continued into adulthood and played a crucial role in my rehabilitation. It started out slowly. A stir and a taste as I passed through the kitchen. "I think that could use some more salt," I would proclaim. Making requests for dinner soon followed: my mom's stuffed bell peppers or beef stew with crispy, bloated biscuits baked right on top, like dumplings. Gazing out the front window, I watched the cars zip home, carrying families and their parcels from the day. I would sit quietly at the kitchen table, gathering the sites and sounds of my mother's dinner preparation. But eventually the sizzle of the onions set to sauté in butter, tempered with olive oil, became tempting; those potatoes crisping in the oven became too delectable to ignore. Dragging my right leg to meet my left, I pushed myself slowly from the kitchen table to the stove. That's where everything really goes on in the kitchen.

My mother was happy to have the company, although initially it made her nervous. She hovered. Cooking with her adult daughter was like cooking with me as a young girl again. She helped me lift platters from shelves and pull pots from the corners of the cabinet. She watched anxiously as I struggled with a chef's knife and a small stack of scallions. I was a lefty now, though I often forgot, as I would place the spindly green onions on the cutting board. I can't tell you how many times I had to switch the vegetable from side to side, then place my deadened right hand on the board, like a stump. It would brace the vegetables and I would begin to chop, very slowly and incredibly carefully. The last thing I needed to do was lose a finger on my strong hand due to some unsightly kitchen accident.

Soon I grew more comfortable, and my mother did, too. Our roles in the kitchen began to reverse. Now she was the one resting at the kitchen table, and I was the one perched, hovering over the stove.

So when Thanksgiving rolled around, that gluttonous holiday that is all about savory turkeys crammed tightly with cornbread stuffing and gooey blankets of toasty brown marshmallow covering bubbly casserole dishes of yams, we were ready. The discussion began in October. "What's on the menu this year?" I asked my mom repeatedly, even though the menu had been basically the same since I was a child.

"Well, the basics for sure, but I also read this recipe for creamed onions in the Julia and Jacques cookbook that sounded tempting."

"Hmm, that sounds good." I could imagine the luscious cream sauce swirling aromatically on each of the diner's plates. "Let's try it out. It might be nice to have something new on the dinner plate."

Of all the holidays, Thanksgiving is my favorite. As autumn tumbles into season, the gearing up begins. We have said good-bye to summer long ago, with its final Labor Day barbecues and bowlfuls of corn salad. Halloween has come and gone, with its marshmallow pumpkins coated in a waxy chocolate and trick-or-treat–size packages of candy. Then there is Thanksgiving.

Come November 1, my mother would break out the candles embellished with pilgrims, and the cornucopias filled with dried ears of corn would adorn the dining room table for the rest of the month. Each week, I would choose a new pimply gourd to bring home from the grocery store, and slowly we would begin to unearth the serving dishes that were only used during the holidays. When I was in school, I always looked forward to this first substantial break from my studies with this celebration of food.

I love how most every American, wherever they may be, eats the same thing, with little bits of variation thrown in to make each person's holiday unique. My sister's roommate from college is Italian. So although her family would have the typical turkey and even a Jell-O salad to boot, they also had large platters of rib-sticking lasagna and plump ravioli. I remember talking about my love for the holiday with Brian early on in our relationship. He mentioned casually that for the past few years his parents had come up from L.A., and he and his sister went to a restaurant with them. I was aghast. "But what about the leftovers? You don't have any leftovers if you go out!" All I can say is that it's a good thing I married him and rescued the in-laws from eating yet another holiday feast out.

The year that I returned home to my parents' house, Thanksgiving was huge. It seemed that a good part of the free world showed up at our house on a brisk Thursday afternoon. So much of my family and friends rallied around us that year. Or perhaps they were treating it as a kind of freak show, each person interested to see how the newly disabled would cope with her meal. I was in charge of some of the sides, leaving the negotiation of a thirty-pound bird to my mom and uncle.

For the green vegetable, I chose to make Brussels sprouts. I love them, and I feel that this adorable little cruciferous vegetable gets a bad rap. It's how you prepare the sprouts that makes them amazing, and I julienned them. Well, actually, since I was still unsteady with a knife, my sister, who doesn't love to cook but cast her preferences aside in the name of holiday cheer, sliced all the Brussels sprouts into neat julienned bundles.

It was getting close to dinnertime. The stove in the kitchen was topped with vats of gravy and double boilers mounded high with mashed potatoes teetering on top of saucepans. The creamed onions were keeping warm in the oven, and I retreated to the laundry room, where an electric frying pan was plugged in on top of the washer. Maia and her mother were among the guests that year, and Maia stood by me among the bottles of detergent, holding open plastic bags filled with the wispy green shreddings. With a wooden spoon, I melted the butter and sautéed the sprouts. I splashed in glugs of cream and seasoned with salt and pepper. I tasted carefully, salted more, then tasted again, enjoying the rhythm.

Cooking & Screaming

The Brussels sprouts were as much a project completed by Maia as they were by me, but for me they meant so much more. That Thanksgiving, the buffet table was full: slices of buttery turkey; stuffing enhanced with onions, celery, and poultry seasoning; fluffy mashed potatoes; saucers full of gravy; yams accented with marshmallows for the traditionalists, and with pecans for the disciples of Martha Stewart were stacked among dishes of condiments. Standing tall, in the silver-plated casserole dish, were my Brussels sprouts. It didn't really matter that some people were too set in their Brussels-sprout-hating ways to give them a try. They were my contribution to the feast and my first opportunity to feed others.

I had struggled with my disability, and the questioning would only continue about where I would stand in this new life. But as it turned out, I did not need to find some resolution before becoming whole once again. I did not need to talk about being a disabled young person. I had looked to David to give me a verbal cure, to my doctors for a time frame for recovery, and to my physical therapists in order to perfect my gait. But I needed to take responsibility for the person I was turning into, and I needed to be active with my body as much as I could be. Sautéing those shards of Brussels sprouts proved to be what I needed. Thanksgiving came at precisely the right moment.

CHAPTER 7

Brown Sugar Angel Food Cake
with Lemon Glaze

When I was young, I had a penchant for angel food cake. Don't ask me why a skinny girl of nine so loved a dietetic cake. I think it was the light texture and sheer volume of a cake this size—such a big cake for such a little girl. Many of my birthday cakes were angel food, lovingly made for me by my mother and tinted pink by the candied sugar sprinkles mixed into the batter.

This angel food cake recipe is unique in its use of brown rather than white sugar. Brown sugar gives a pleasing color (though not quite as festive as the pink) and a subtle molasses flavor. I have also included a recipe for a simple lemon glaze. This is a slightly different, more mature cake that still reminds me of birthdays.

FOR THE CAKE:
1¼ cups sifted cake flour
2 cups firmly packed brown
   sugar
1½ cups egg whites (10–12
   eggs)
1½ teaspoons cream of
   tartar
1 teaspoon salt

2 teaspoons vanilla extract
Zest of 1 lemon

FOR THE GLAZE:
1½ cups confectioners' sugar
¼ cup lemon juice
   (2 medium-size lemons)
½ teaspoon vanilla extract

Preheat the oven to 350°F. Combine the cake flour and 1 cup of the brown sugar in a medium-size bowl and set aside. In a large bowl, beat the egg whites with the cream of tartar and salt until foamy. Continue beating the egg whites while slowly adding the remaining cup of brown sugar. This takes about 5 minutes. The egg whites should be glossy and stiff upon completion. Add the vanilla extract and lemon zest; blend well.

Divide the flour–brown sugar mixture into four portions. Using a large rubber spatula, fold each portion into the meringue separately by gently lifting the meringue up and rolling it over. Fold until no traces of dry ingredients can be seen, but the batter is still light in texture. Gently pour the batter into an ungreased 10-inch tube (angel food cake) pan with a rubber spatula. With a long, sharp knife, make five or six vertical cuts through the batter to eliminate any large air pockets.

Bake for 45–50 minutes, or until the top of the cake springs back after it is touched lightly with a finger. Remove from the oven and immediately invert the pan. If the pan does not have legs, place the center tube over the neck of a large, heavy bottle. Do not remove the cake from the pan until it is completely cool. This takes at least 1 hour. To release the cake from the pan, create air pockets by easing a sharp knife around the perimeter. You may have to do this several times.

Once the cake is cooled and removed from the pan, make the glaze. In a bowl, sift the confectioners' sugar over the lemon juice and add the vanilla extract. Stir well to create a smooth, lump-free glaze. Spoon the glaze over the top of the cake, letting the glaze flow down the sides of the cake. The glaze will harden in 1 hour.

serves 12

Slow Cooking

For two long years, therapy was my life. I saw it as a job that I went to, five days a week. I was raised with a strong work ethic—that is, you went to work even when it was beautiful outside and the only thing you could think of was languishing near some body of water. And so I threw myself into therapy. Throughout this time, my parents were steadfast. They had experienced a similar struggle following my father's stroke, first in overcoming his paralysis and then continuously confronting his speech issues. They understood the devastating blow that had occurred to me both physically and emotionally. They also understood that it took time. To feel normal again, to be normal again, whatever that was. At home, I didn't need to have an explanation of where I was going with my life. My parents just let me be.

Yet my lifestyle was an embarrassment to me, a looming, undisguiseable secret that I wasn't even sure how to discuss with new people. Brian and I would find ourselves at parties, and while he was off being both amusing and entertaining, I would be quaking in my sensible boots, awaiting the dreaded question: "So what do you do, Adrienne?"

I think that in order to excel in social situations modesty must be chucked out the window. You cannot be self-conscious. To be a good guest, you must be witty, charming, and helpful. Which I can easily be with close friends; but sit me in a room of strangers around a bowl of mediocre guacamole, and I freeze.

"Well," I would begin my tirade, laughing nervously. "I do massive amounts of therapy. Not the mental health sort, but pretty much every other kind you can think of. You see, I had an AVM. Do you know what that is? It's fine if you don't—I mean, I had never heard of them—that is, before mine ruptured. It's like a stroke." I would glance at my conversation partner, who would be staring blankly. "I know, scary, right? So I'm pretty much trying to rehabilitate myself. . . . That's it."

Okay . . .

Hadn't I heard of the phrase "too much information"? Not everyone needed to know the neuroses of my everyday life. I learned this fairly quickly as people at parties backed away from the gimpy girl standing next to the onion dip. As I grew more comfortable with my life, I learned to say, "Actually, I'm unemployed right now," while hiding my right arm behind my torso. And that was enough; everyone's been unemployed at some time in their life, and so we would move on to the next topic of conversation.

At graduation there are many air kisses, messy smacks turned into civilized pursed-lip gesticulations in the general direction of the fleshy part of the face. There are lots of forced and thankful good-byes to acquaintances who sat in your English 1B class, always in the third row, lost in the center of the classroom. There are the people who you swear to keep in touch with as soon as they return from their graduation trip to Turkey and then you never see them again after that chilly May morning when you march together to "Pomp and Circumstance." And then there are the people who you celebrate with, exclaiming, "We're finally finished!" only to meet the very next morning over coffee to nurse your respective hangovers from an evening of carousing and wicked celebration.

I did not have the traditional cap and gown graduation; I did not walk with my fellow classmates in the Greek Theater of Berkeley that spring. But word of my fate caught on like a game of operator in a second-grade classroom. I had friends who were dumbfounded yet rushed to the hospital, expecting for me to wake up and then our friendships would carry on having suffered this minor glitch. There were friends who heard the news and took it as a dirty little piece of gossip. They would whisper about me at parties: "Oh, have you heard about Adrienne? A stroke, I think . . . twenty-one. I know, can you believe it?" Those friends disappeared, like the gossip they were carrying. They took that salacious bit of knowledge about my life and scurried away. I guess my AVM was intriguing for them to talk about, but having a crippled friend was too much to deal with. Then there were people who came out of the recesses of my past. I had a small passel of devastation groupies. They were old friends, ex-boyfriends, those same groups of acquaintances from English 1B. People whom I didn't really feel like seeing were now sending me large arrangements of gerbera daisies with that sorry excuse for a filler flower, baby's breath. I guess it's the thought that counts, but let's be honest here.

One of my oldest and truest friends was Jane, a girl I had met singing around campfires and swatting mosquitoes from our shoulders at summer camp. It was a quiet Saturday afternoon at Vallejo. The doctors had gone home for the weekend, the nurses were on skeleton crew, and Jane came to see me carrying a very large knapsack. She sat down near my bed and unzipped the bag. Out popped her scrawny Chihuahua's head, like a furry apple. Jane knew that I needed the pure love of a dog to offer an escape from my surroundings.

Jane was my friend without an internal dialogue, a lover of Oprah—the Doctor Phil years—and self-help books of all kinds. She was always good for a story, usually involving her wacky family, her latest theory on love, and kabbalah or some other trendy religion. For all of her loopy wanderings, her utter lack of pretense was refreshing in my world of new college graduates, each out to impress their peers with their worldly knowledge.

Jane picked me up to take me out for lunch some months after I was released from Vallejo. It was two o'clock, after the lunch rush of hungry noontime diners. I pushed away my plate of a half-eaten tuna melt, cheese congealing in a slick mass underneath the grilled sourdough toast. "So what's it like?" Jane asked directly.

"What's what like?"

"Being you now. How does it feel? To be, for lack of a better word—disabled. Or whatever it is that *you* want to call it. I mean, it must be pretty intense."

Coming from anyone else this question might have seemed intrusive, but this was Jane, simply asking me a question, much like the waitress had done a half hour earlier when she came by our table to take our order. This was the question I had been waiting for. The question I felt that I would be answering for the rest of my life. The question I *wanted* to have an answer for—I really did. But it was almost too looming of a question for me to approach.

"It *is* intense . . . I don't know."

"I'm sorry. Was that too personal? It's kind of amazing, to be one way your entire existence, and then, *whoosh*," she said, finger tickling the air, "you're another."

"Yeah, I guess it is sort of amazing," I said, pushing my body away from the table and struggling to rise and balance on my two legs, although my right leg seemed to have checked out. "Should we go?"

"Okay," Jane replied, but I was hurrying out the door ahead of her, or hurrying out as much as a one-armed, one-legged cripple could hurry.

That night, as I lay wide awake in the same bed where only weeks before I had achieved what was becoming the unthinkable, raising my arm high above my head, I replayed Jane's question over and over. It was hard to believe that this *was* my life now: being driven to a myriad of appointments by random members of my family like a teenager waiting to get her driver's license. There was the physical therapist, the occupational therapist, the speech therapist, the *therapist* therapist. No longer could I scamper up stairs; the elevator was now my friend. I was twenty-two years old and the stairs were not kind to me. My birthday came and went, hardly noticeable.

But had I truly suffered? Suffering was starving, and I ate plentifully. Suffering was being maimed, and I was whole, intact, though not always functioning. Suffering was losing a loved one; I had lost no one. Yes, suffering could be much worse than what I dealt with on a daily basis. Yet, I felt something down deep in the recesses of my newly morphed body; it was a sadness that was hard to touch. I was in mourning. Mourning for an old life; mourning for my once-active limbs.

In college, I had read about grief and mourning. The final stage is acceptance, preceded by denial, anger, and depression. Where was I in this grand scheme of things? As I lay in bed that night, tears welling in my eyes, the darkness hiding much more than my body in my bed, I knew that I had not reached that ultimate stage yet.

Dr. Morris, the speech pathologist who due to unfortunate circumstances worked with both my father and now me, lived near the beach in a newish tract home not far from a charming older section of Half Moon Bay. At times we would meet at her house, which mysteriously smelled of wet dog, and other times she would drive down to the peninsula, where we would close ourselves in a spare room at my parents' office, my own work still ahead. But I loved driving to Half Moon Bay.

The car chugged upward until it reached the crest of the hills, and there the ocean would be, a blanket of blue under a gray sky smeared with clouds. It never really mattered how warm it was on the other side of the mountains—you would always need a sweater by the ocean.

During the drive we would pass the nurseries selling annuals and perennials, and the abandoned pumpkin patches, boarded up until the following Halloween when they would once again be filled with riotous children. The air was heavy and thick with the scents of the ocean. When I was young, my father used to take me "fishing" off the Princeton pier, the next town over from Half Moon Bay. My father didn't know the first thing about fishing, or the ocean for that matter, but he bought two cheap rods at the drugstore with the intention of learning. They hung, leering over us in the garage, waiting to be claimed and used on weekend fishing expeditions.

My father is an early riser, so waking up at 6:00 A.M. on a Saturday was nothing for him. Getting his daughter to do the same was a trial. But lured from bed by the promise of donuts and hot cocoa, I would quickly dress and we would head out. Perched at the edge of the pier, donut in one hand, fishing rod in the other, my dad and I would spend a few hours talking and trying to stay warm in the damp morning fog. Stabbing live wiggly worms with the notched hook made me squeamish, and we never caught anything worth mentioning, let alone anything substantial enough to take home and fry up, but the drive to Half Moon Bay, with the drone of the news station on the radio in the background, always meant time shared with my father. Now, this same trip meant that I was on my way to yet another therapy session.

When I was released from Vallejo, I was given a clean bill of health, mentally and cognitively. But I didn't feel that way. I had had a brain hemorrhage; *blood* had seeped into parts of my brain, affecting movement and motor skills. It didn't seem possible that these were the only parts affected. I was taking large doses of an antiseizure medication. In addition to preventing seizures, the drug works by generally slowing all of the body's functions, producing side effects like sluggish metabolism, dizziness, fatigue, and general malaise. For the months that I was on the medication, I walked around feeling like a bloated zombie.

As trying as the physical struggles of rehabilitation were, the mental difficulties were by far the most challenging. I was living in a dim world. I had graduated from college; my friends were beginning to choose careers for themselves, to use their education wisely. I longed to do the same. No one even noticed my aphasia, but it was something that I was particularly sensitive to. Here I was, at the brink of starting my life, yet living in a bubble. There were things that I wanted to say, but it was as though I was verbally stifled. Words would go floating by me, each in a bubble of its own, and I felt unable to pop *my* bubble, to set free a cascade of words. I was unwilling to waste the last four years of my life. I would not be destined to a life of monosyllabic words.

So my parents called Dr. Morris, who had been assisting my dad in rehabilitation for years. Many months later, I watched her from across her dining room table. She pored over pamphlets of old homework assignments antiqued by years of use, and I waited for her to come up with the one sheet of paper that would solve all of my word-finding dilemmas, the needle with which to pop the bubble. I was frustrated. Dr. Morris was experienced with global aphasias—the inability to communicate in depth—but I was not entirely convinced that she knew what to do with me, even though *I* couldn't express to her what I needed.

She would give me brief writing assignments that I would plunk out, left-handed, on the keyboard in the evenings. I would glance down at her neat, cursive, teacher-like script: *Write one paragraph about your family.* Or: *Tell me about a favorite trip you have taken and why.* Come on! I was twenty-two years old, not twelve, but I would write the minimum, briefly answering the question, and starting each paragraph with the always thoughtful "I."

One night, after finishing dinner and listening to the subtle clinking of my father doing the dishes down the hall in the kitchen, I looked down at my homework assignment: *Write about a favorite birthday and why.* Now I had had some memorable birthdays, that's for sure. There was my sweet sixteen surprise party—sort of—when I found all of the invitations in my sister's purse weeks before the celebration. And my twenty-first birthday in Las Vegas, where I played one hand of poker in the casino, got bored, and then delightedly people-watched the rest of the weekend. But those were not the birthdays I chose to write about. Instead, I wrote:

> Birthdays came twofold in my house. I had an intimate party, with just the family on the actual day, and the blowout party on the weekend. Having a birthday in October meant one thing to me—a Halloween fête. While other kids had parties at the roller-skating rink after school, or at the movies on the weekend, I always had a craft-oriented birthday party at the house, on a Saturday afternoon. One year we made witches' masks out of egg cartons; another year we decorated mini-pumpkins with glitter, puffs of yarn, and tacky craft glue; and another still, we constructed Halloween wreaths from foil garlands of ghosts. But regardless of what Halloween-oriented craft was made each year, one thing remained the same—I got to select what was on the menu for that Saturday afternoon. My birthday—my menu. And it changed every year.
>
> The year of "filayasole" was a favorite for me. I must have been

turning seven. Sometime in September, my mother reminded me of my impending birthday (as if a reminder was even necessary). It was time for me to start thinking of what I wanted to serve. Mashed potatoes were a given—that homey, starchy goodness was a perennial favorite. I knew that I had to select a vegetable, and that year I was a big fan of broccoli—don't ask me why—so that sulfuric vegetable went on the menu, too. And last but not least, I informed my mom that I wanted "filayasole." And, oh yes, an angel food cake with whipped cream and strawberries, no matter that it wasn't truly strawberry season, for my big birthday cake.

"Filayasole? I don't know that I know what that is," my mom replied cautiously.

"Sure you do. We had it last week. It's that stuff that you dip in flour and then fry up. The fish."

My mom smirked, and soon the smirk turned into laughter. "You mean *fillet of sole*. It's three separate words. Fillet. Of. Sole."

"Whatever. That's what I want."

And that is what was served at my party that October. Mild, flaky white fish at a kid's birthday. What can I say? I knew what was good.

WHEN I TURNED in my homework assignment to Dr. Morris the following week, I watched a smile of recognition appear on her face. "Well, this is wonderful. I can see what you're capable of and that I probably have been giving you the wrong type of work in our sessions."

Our sessions were better from that point on. I needed to open up more, to tell my therapist what I wanted to truly achieve. I learned that combating my aphasia was a struggle of wills, as well as a struggle of language. There would be times when speaking would seem too difficult; plucking words out of oblivion to make a sentence was rough. Conversation became a form of education for me. At times I would get lazy, asking myself: *Does this really need to be said? How necessary is my contribution to the conversation?* And for this English major with a mouth on her that always got her into trouble while growing up, and as someone who enjoyed conversations with others, the answer was always that my contribution to conversations was very necessary.

From that day on, Dr. Morris and I talked about food and childhood and family—the only subjects that I felt equipped to speak about at length. She told me about a sheet cake that she makes from fruit cocktail (you will never see me making that), and I even gave her the filayasole recipe.

CHAPTER 8

Sage and Parmesan Popcorn

I always forget how much I love popcorn—the homemade kind to be exact. There is something so tempting about the clamorous pinging of the corn kernels against the lid of a saucepan. And when it's still warm, seasoned with butter, salt, really anything you like, it can't be beat. Remembering my after-school hunger, I thought that it would be the ideal snack to offer a teenager whom I was wrangled into tutoring. I'm not sure if she appreciated the snack food, but I'm pretty sure that what she did not appreciate was having to visit a tutor at all.

This recipe is for a decidedly grown-up popcorn. Seasoned with sage and Parmesan cheese, it's the perfect snack to accompany cocktails or a tutoring session.

2 tablespoons vegetable or canola oil	¾ cup finely grated Parmesan cheese
⅓ cup popcorn kernels	½ teaspoon salt
1 tablespoon unsalted butter	½ teaspoon pepper
1 tablespoon minced fresh sage	

In a large, lidded saucepan, over medium-high heat, add the oil and popcorn kernels. Cover the saucepan, then begin gently shaking the pan over the heat. The movement prevents the kernels from scorching. Listen for the pinging of the kernels, after 4–5 minutes, and continue shaking the pan until the pinging slows and all of the kernels are popped. Remove the lid and pour the popcorn into a large bowl or a clean brown paper bag.

Wipe out the saucepan, turn the heat to low, and add the butter. Melt the butter, and as the foam subsides, add the sage. Continue cooking for an additional 30 seconds, until the sage crisps. Add the butter and sage mixture to the popcorn, along with the Parmesan cheese, salt, and pepper. Toss well to evenly distribute. Taste for seasoning and serve.

makes approximately 10 cups

Brain Food

There is a picture that I drew on cheap grade-school paper when I was five years old—a pictogram of Adrienne through the ages. There are several small depictions of me: in infancy, bundled snuggly in a blanket; in elementary school, with posts growing from the side of my head, which I assume are supposed to be pigtails; a girl carrying a stack of books—that's me in college; and lastly, a lean line drawing of me standing in front of a matte green rectangle, a chalkboard, the mature me. I was all grown up, and I was a teacher.

I never had dreams of my wedding. The poufy dress never appealed to me; I did not longingly dote on my imaginary prince charming. The wedding cake, an astounding multilayered confection—now *that* appealed to me, but for different reasons. That is not to say that I never thought about my future. I always imagined that I would become a teacher. Dashing off to school, bringing piles of grading home with me, and summers off—the life of a teacher seemed perfect. I would be the cool teacher, like my high school English teacher Ms. Holiday. With long, wiry gray hair and cool cat-eye glasses, she played Lou Reed albums while we were working quietly at our desks, and it was rumored that she had a poem published in *Rolling Stone* that was all about men's ejaculation. Yes, I would be like Ms. Holiday.

This dream stayed with me well into college. Attending Berkeley meant that I would be a complete product of a public school education, a badge I wore with a certain element of pride. As my friends in college decided on majors and thought of what they would do with the rest of their lives, I knew. I would major in English, and I would become a high school English teacher. I was so sure of this decision; I never gave it a second thought. While my friends were constantly questioning their decisions, I found comfort in the stability of my own. But when my life was turned upside down that month of my graduation, I started to truly ask myself questions. Was teaching what I wanted to do? How could *I* impart knowledge when now it seemed that life was full of unanswerable questions? If I did go into teaching, I would be forever known as the crippled teacher. Was I ready for that scrutiny?

The one-year anniversary of my AVM was quickly approaching, and with each passing month, college seemed more like a distant memory and having a life as a teacher seemed more unattainable.

"I have a job for you," Aunt Claire said on the phone one evening. "I have a friend with a teenage daughter, Tamar, who could use a little assistance in the English department. It's not that her grades are miserable; it's that she has some trouble grasping the bigger picture. Or at least that's what George says. He is looking for a tutor for her, and I immediately thought of you! You should call him. He's expecting you."

Aunt Claire did not let up. We spoke or saw each other on a regular basis, and it was as if she didn't see me. We would discuss the daily monotonies of our lives, mine being traveling to see one therapist or another, but Aunt Claire refused to acknowledge how I was doing physically. She would only speak of the future, which for her was my fledgling teaching career. Aunt Claire was a hungry dog with a bone. She held on to that one morsel of information I imparted to her when I was younger and shook it with such tenacity that she would make me become a teacher. "Adrienne, what do you think?"

"I'll give him a call. Thanks for the opportunity." Aunt Claire absolutely meant well, but she wasn't even trying to understand what it was like for a twenty-one-year-old's life to change entirely. Then again, perhaps I was being too hasty in my decision *not* to become a teacher. Maybe the reason that I couldn't envision myself in front of the classroom was because I had been away from a school environment for close to a year. Maybe tutoring would be a way to inch myself back into school. Maybe I would find that the AVM was a bump in the road and teaching was indeed what I truly wanted to do with my life. I could do this.

SITTING AT THE kitchen table, I alternated between staring out the front window and lamely readying myself for my very first tutoring session. I straightened my pencils, stacked my notebooks neatly, and snacked on the freshly popped popcorn kernels one by one that I had made for a snack. Even if she hated me as a tutor, Tamar would at least return for the snacks. Popcorn had always been a mainstay in my house, and not the sunny yellow butter-flavored microwavable kind. My mom made popcorn the old-fashioned way, kernels in steaming hot oil. The large saucepan actually had dings and scorch marks left behind from the popping kernels. *Ting, pop, pop, ting*, as the kernels bounced against the lid of the saucepan, they announced their arrival.

A car pulled up in the driveway and rolled to a stop in front of the house. It was a small convertible with an unpronounceable German name—we used to call them bitch baskets when I was in high school, because they were: dinged slightly, most-likely used, with a roll bar, making them look remarkably like baskets. Boys never drove these cars; if they did, surely they would go by another name. I watched as the driver glanced at her reflection in the rearview mirror, pulling tendrils from her messy pony-tail down to frame her face. Her long legs extended out of the basket. She was wearing short soccer shorts, emblazoned with her school's name across the butt. I could tell that her legs were smoothly shaven, the kind of shaving that requires time and patience as you repeatedly go over the same strip of leg on your calf, the kind of shave that I have never achieved. She scampered to the front door and rang the bell. So this was my tutee.

"Hi, you must be Tamar. I'm Adrienne," I said, extending my left hand.

"Yeah, hi. It's nice to meet you," Tamar said, removing her left hand from the front pocket of her hoodie sweatshirt.

"Well, come in. I figured we could sit and talk for a minute. Get to know each other. You can tell me a bit about yourself, what you're expecting from me, anything you want to know in particular . . ."

"Okay."

Tamar was definitely a teenager. Beside the fact that the name of her high school was written boldly across her derriere, her body was mature. She had outgrown her gangly limbs, but as she stood before me, fists punching the inside of her sweatshirt, it was clear that she was still unsure of what to do with herself. Pulling a tiny pot of lip balm from her pocket, she glided it on for what would be the first of many times during our hour-and-a-half session together.

"Here, do you want some popcorn? I just made it."

"Sure," Tamar said, plunging her hand, fingernails bitten to the quick, into the bowl. "Well, I'm not even too sure why I'm here. I mean, I do fine in English. A's and B's. But my dad says I'm not learning enough, so here I am."

Clearly, getting a tutor was not Tamar's idea. And it was becoming clear that she was only sitting at the kitchen table at my parents' house, messily snacking on popcorn, because her father told her to. "Okay, well let's make the best of the situation," I said. "There must be something that you have questions about or that you feel like you could use *some* assistance with."

"No."

"Well, what are you reading for school right now?"

Tamar reached into her bag—a large, woven straw satchel. "This," she said, pushing a tattered copy of Annie Dillard's *The Writing Life* across the table.

I smirked. "Oh my god, are they still giving you this to read?" Thumbing through the pages, I recalled how amazingly dry I thought this work was. At the age of sixteen, I could not relate to the musings of a middle-age recluse, and now, as I looked at this book again, I knew that there must be a more useful book out there from which to learn. The book is slim, maybe a hundred pages, but it reads like one giant hundred-page five-paragraph essay, with a thesis, supporting paragraphs, and a tight conclusion. I tried to let my opinion remain neutral and see what Tamar had to say about the prose. "Have you started reading it?"

Tamar nodded. "I don't read much; it's not really my thing. But it's good—for a schoolbook."

And that was pretty much how the following few weeks went. Tamar would drive up to the front of my house and begrudgingly get out of her bitch basket. Most days she was almost mute, answering the questions I asked her in monosyllables. At first, I took her general disinterest to mean that she was shy, but as the tutoring sessions progressed and her attitude did not alter, I was beginning to think the apathy was simply Tamar.

We read together, talked about what we had read—I reread *The Writing Life* and still didn't like it. Together we worked on Tamar's expository writing assignments for school. I even gave her my own writing assignments, which I am sure were very popular with her. To be fair, Tamar never complained. She always completed the assignments, but as she handed me crumpled pages, torn out of her spiral-bound notebook, I knew that she hated her homework. Now I knew how Dr. Morris must have felt. I tried everything; I even found essays that were not about writing but were focused on sports or athletics. These essays expounded on the joys of acing a goal or the camaraderie of being a member of a team—something I never found interesting but that I figured the girl sitting across the table from me wearing shin guards and knee-high socks would. But it was no use. As each week passed, I found that the one thing I could count on from my tutoring sessions was the increasing feeling of gloom, which I'm sure was equally felt by my tutee. Tamar's disinterest was infectious. And my own little experiment, my venture into the world of teaching, was blowing up in my face.

During my senior year of college, my mother taught me how to knit. It was the very beginning of the knitting craze, when you would see gaggles of women gabbing over their knitting needles at local coffeehouses. I imagined myself knitting cozy sweaters or a scarf so long it need not be limited to your neck and could be wrapped around your entire body. So I learned. I went to yarn shops and discussed the benefits of bamboo over metal needles with the patrons. I bought yarn and books. But a few weeks later, sitting on my living room sofa amid all of my knitting paraphernalia, I found I didn't really love to knit. In fact, I wasn't even sure I liked it. Well, that was sort of what happened with teaching and Tamar. How had Ms. Holiday made *The Tempest*, a play she had read and taught countless times, seem interesting to a room full of fifteen-year-olds, most of whom would only read the Cliffs Notes anyway? I assumed that being a teacher was a noble and selfless job—two attributes that I could not find within myself at this point in time.

Maybe I had thought about teaching for so long without ever really trying it out that I automatically thought it was the only thing I could do. Seeing Tamar every week was like visiting high school all over again, and I wasn't sure that I liked it. I happily had not had disparaging thoughts about girls growing into suburban wives wearing mom jeans in years. With Tamar's presence, I had those thoughts weekly. I knew that there was an entire world of careers to try. Driving with my mom, I would pass the people on their way to work each day. Sleepy people talking on their cell phones or fiddling with something in their lap, these employees were my peers, but belted into the passenger seat next to my mom, I felt as if I were on a different planet from them. Their lives were full of careers, bosses, meeting for drinks after work, while my life was filled with therapy, doctors, and now, a sullen teenager who was sent to see me each week because her father made her.

Maia had since moved to New York City to pursue a career in publishing. Brian was back at Berkeley attending graduate school in music composition. And I was happy for their pursuits. Their lives were continuing, but my life was stagnant. There had to be more than just therapy. Maybe that is what Aunt Claire was telling me by prodding me into teaching. Tutoring Tamar turned out to be an educational disappointment for me. I was finding that perhaps I did not want to spend my days surrounded by girls in soccer shorts. But discovering my preferences was terrifying. I asked the question that all graduates ask themselves: What do you want to do with the rest of your life? I had been derailed from figuring out the answer to this important question while I was consumed with rehabilitation. Now I could feel it lurking, and as much as I tried, I knew that it could not be ignored.

CHAPTER 9

Not Your Father's Three-Bean Salad

Three-bean salad is one of my father's favorites, but all the beans taste the same to me. Drowning in brine, a garbanzo bean is indiscriminate from a kidney bean, which is indiscriminate from a green bean (which is really gray). The idea of a three-bean salad is nice; it is just the way that these beans cohabitate together that rubs me the wrong way. I want my salads bright and clean, with crunch and interest. So that is what you will find in this three-bean salad. The garbanzo beans are roasted, making them substantial and meaty; the lima beans are buttery and rich (I opted out of the usual kidney beans); and the green beans are crisp-tender. Throw in some torn bits of toasted bread for added crunch, and there you have it. It's not my dad's usual three-bean salad—it's better.

15-ounce can garbanzo
   beans, drained
3 cups bite-size pieces of
   bread—French or Italian,
   like baguette or ciabatta
   (day-old is fine)
4 tablespoons olive oil
salt and pepper to taste
1 cup frozen lima beans
1 cup green or flat beans, cut
   into ¾-inch pieces

3 canned oil-cured anchovy
   fillets, rinsed
2 tablespoons fresh lemon
   juice
Zest of 1 lemon
1 tablespoon white wine
   vinegar
¼ cup chopped fresh flat-leaf
   parsley

Preheat the oven to 350°F. In a shallow baking pan, toss the garbanzo beans and bread in 1 tablespoon of olive oil, salt, and pepper. Roast the mixture in the oven for 20–25 minutes until the bread begins to get toasty and the garbanzo beans become firm.

Set a medium-size pot of salted water to boil. Boil the lima beans until tender, 4–5 minutes. Remove them from the water with a slotted spoon and set to completely dry. In the same pot of boiling water, cook the green beans until they are crisp-tender, 2–3 minutes. Remove them from the water and rinse well in cold water to stop the cooking process. Then dry them thoroughly.

With the back of a knife, crush the anchovy fillets. In a small saucepan, over medium heat, blend the anchovies and the remaining olive oil. When the olive oil begins to bubble, turn off the heat and add the lemon juice, lemon zest, and vinegar, stirring well to emulsify.

In a large bowl, combine the beans and bread, pour over the dressing, add the parsley, and toss well. Taste for seasoning and serve.

serves 4–6

Big Food

His hands were always warm, no matter the season. In the winter, I would stuff my little hands into the pocket of his gray London Fog coat and find his hand laying wide open, awaiting my tiny paw. His palm was soft and welcoming, and I would curl my fingers, which had become numb and frostbitten, around his craggy fingers. He would squeeze gently, sometimes kneading the palm of my hand like a piece of dough, and we would walk together, my little arm embracing his big one. My dad was not a big man, but he was an imposing figure. With icy, silver curls, a potbelly, and a kind face, my dad was larger than life, which was fitting considering what he did for a living.

Making giant inflatables—and by inflatables I mean those enormous passengerless blimps flying above used car lots, and King Kong–like creatures ferociously growling on the top of a building near the freeway—seems like a fanciful business, filled with imagination and wonder . . . and it was. It was also a business like any other, filled with sales figures, demographics, and profit/loss sheets. And Pie in the Sky, or PITS as it was later and more disparagingly known, was a true family business, with my mother running production, my father handling all the sales and marketing, and my sister, when she graduated from college, doing all the work in between.

Pie in the Sky was my parents' bread and butter. It never occurred to me that what they did for a living was so unusual—until one day, when the conversation at the school cafeteria table inevitably turned to what your parents did for a living. Some children's parents were doctors, lawyers, teachers, and a few kids didn't really know what their parents did. Then I said, "They manufacture large inflatable balloons, blimps, and product replicas for outdoor advertising purposes." The moment my classmates stopped chewing their peanut butter and jelly sandwiches, that was when I sort of knew.

For career day, my dad brought the especially amazing balloons to school. On the soccer field, he set up a twenty-foot-long chameleon, its nylon tongue flapping loosely in front of it. Kids would ooh and aah, asking if they could touch it and if my dad had more of these at home. I was proud, thinking, *Look what my parents do. Everyone else will go home to their boring parents and talk about this over dinner.* Then I would slip my hand into my dad's welcoming one.

My dad was a family man who loved his girls fiercely, but he was also a workaholic. To him, life was all about Pie in the Sky and his family. My mother was the grounding force behind the inflatable empire, leading to an even more intricate tangling of interests. When my dad met my mom, a warm, insightful, clear-headed woman, I imagine that when he looked at her in her Pucci-style mini-dress and saucer-shaped sunglasses, he saw a rich life. They were married three weeks after they met. My mom has always said that although she did not know my father well at this point—she may not have known his favorite foods or how he liked his toast in the morning—she knew that they would have an interesting life together. And she believed in all that my father had to offer. That trust was exactly what my dad needed. They eloped to Las Vegas, so when Brian and I got married in a small civil ceremony, I like to think that I was keeping with tradition.

Following my parents' wedding, my mother moved from San Francisco into my father's apartment in Los Angeles. It was virtually empty when she arrived. There was a tattered sofa, a stiff set of dining chairs surrounding a dusty glass-topped table, and a handful of chipped dishes in a drying rack near the kitchen sink. The refrigerator door sighed softly from lack of use, and when my mother opened it, she saw a handful of puzzling items to a girl raised in the Midwest. There was a loaf of dark Jewish rye bread, one brick of half-eaten cream cheese, and a tube of anchovy paste curled up like a tube of toothpaste. It seemed that my father had been making himself palettes of briny sandwiches, awaiting my mother's arrival. Needless to say, this was the last time my father enjoyed his peculiar sandwich of spreads. My mom came into his life and his bachelor pad, refreshing, like the first sweet lick of an ice-cream cone on a warm summer's night.

My sister, a roly-poly baby with a shock of curls, was born in Los Angeles, but eventually my parents settled in the suburbs of San Francisco to be close to family. I came along six years after my sister, and together, the four of us settled into a calm, stable life. My parents did a good job of making my childhood an idyllic one. I remember sitting at my seat at the kitchen table doing homework while my mom sat at the head of the table doing her homework as well, balancing the checkbooks or doing payroll for the business, an immediacy about her fingers clicking against the plastic keys of the adding machine. I remember always taking winter trips abroad, because the balloon business was a vaguely seasonal one. No one really thinks about outdoor advertising in the frigid winter months. I remember my father's utter lack of interest in sports, either watching or playing. Each Super Bowl Sunday, when it seemed the rest of the American population was glued to their television sets, rooting for their teams, wearing commemorative jerseys, and chomping on chicken wings, my family would go to Golden Gate Park or the Japanese Tea Gardens and eat dim sum in the Richmond district of San Francisco, taking advantage of the lack of people. My parents fit together; there was interest and conversation, joy and laughter.

It seems odd to write these words about my father in the past tense, because he is very much alive. It's just that he is an entirely different man from the father I once knew. In 1995, Christmas weekend to be exact, my father suffered his first debilitating stroke. I was seventeen years old, and life as I knew it changed.

For many years, my family kept up a good front. My mother was now the ringleader of the clan. Friends and extended family would say, "You're so strong—I don't know if I could do it," and my favorite, the hollow, "Let me know if there is anything I can do," when they were actually thinking, *My god, I'm glad that's not me.* We were becoming such experts at playing the game that everything was fine that I don't think anyone really took the time to mourn. We still had my father—for which I am eternally grateful—but he was different and continues to grow more different with each passing day. Now, some thirteen years and several strokes later, he is a shell of the man I grew up with. There is a part of me that mourns the loss of my father every day. I mourn for my mother, who lost her best friend too soon, and I mourn for my sister and me, who did not have the chance to truly know my father when we were adults.

But immediately following my father's first stroke, there was no time for mourning. My mother and my sister carried on with Pie in the Sky, and rehabilitation became my father's full-time occupation. My sister, newly graduated from college, was working at Pie in the Sky until she decided what she wanted to do with her life. She was taking advantage of all my dad had to teach her, and when he had his stroke, her teacher vanished. Instead of leaving PITS and her education coming to a halt, she took over the sales and marketing of the business at the age of twenty-two: trial by fire.

For me, just finishing up high school, the parent who had been a loving caregiver to me was now a needy care receiver. There was a role reversal. My afternoons were spent taking my dad to various appointments, carting him home, and helping my mom. This world of ten-foot inflatable submarine sandwiches and penguins looming forty feet tall was my father's dream, and by carrying on with PITS, I think that my mother was able to hold on to that creative piece of my father, the part that believed anything was possible, for one moment longer. My parents had created a united front, yet half of that pair was now missing.

• • •

It seems that some people are born fully formed; their preferences in place and their reactions set. Others are malleable; they take time to grow into themselves. My father was certainly the former. My father's mother passed away before my parents got married, leaving stacks of yellowed photographs from his past that remained tucked away in boxes until my parents were married and my mother found them. Through those boxes, she came to know my father by asking him to explain the people in the photos and the locales where they were taken. On his first birthday that they shared together, she presented him with an album, each photograph encapsulated with the appropriate anecdote.

When I was growing up, this orange leatherette album was lined up alongside all of our other family albums. On Sunday afternoons, usually in an act of homework procrastination, I would sit on the living room floor, legs outstretched, and thumb through my father's album, marveling at the pictures from his childhood. I saw that my five-year-old father had the same glint in his eyes that he had when I would stand silently in the doorway of his office watching him twirl a piece of Scotch tape between his fingers, going on about how inflatables are a smart advertising choice to a customer on the telephone.

As a young boy, my father lived in Mexico for a few years. His mother had divorced his father and remarried a ranch owner who lived in Guanajuato. Moving there and being surrounded by actual cowboys was a dream come true for a five-year-old with the spirit of a cowboy himself. There is one photograph from this time that is my favorite. Taken in the middle of the afternoon, he is standing in the town square beside a bougainvillea bush so vibrant and in bloom that you can almost see the papery fuchsia buds despite the black-and-white photography. Wearing lederhosen-like shorts, my father has such a look of glee and abandon. He is happy to be alone on this spring day, with no one to answer to. From this young age, this was who he was. He was fully formed. His single-minded independence is the attribute that follows him through his life both pre- and poststroke.

But for all of my father's independence, he is ultimately a creature of habit, one who feels most comfortable with daily routine. I think that was the way he mediated all of the upheaval in his life. Six days a week, my dad awoke at a time many considered to still be night and headed to the office. The life of a workaholic.

My father's bedtime was similar to mine when I was a child. We would climb into bed together at 9:00 P.M. Reading some Judy Blume novel, I would occupy my mother's side of the bed and my father would grab one of the countless newspapers or news magazines that littered my parents' bedroom floor like a glossy side rug. I never remember my father reading novels, but he quickly devoured every piece of journalistic text that was available. As the minutes ticked by, each magazine adequately read, the lids of my dad's eyes would grow heavy. He would switch off his light, signaling to me it was time for bed, before grabbing the earphone dangling delicately beside his clock radio. He plunked it in his ear so that the news station could whisper headlines to him while he slumbered. As my father snored peacefully and exhaustedly, I slept tucked like a mouse on my mother's side of the bed, the scent of her perfume on the gossamer sheets. I would stay like this until my mother nudged me into wakefulness, telling me it was time to go to sleep in my own bed. Through this nightly routine, my father taught me that there is joy to be found in quotidian rituals and beauty in habitual activities.

After my father's stroke, new routines were quickly learned. As they say, old habits die hard, and if your habit is having habits, well, those die even harder. His world no longer revolved around Pie in the Sky; it revolved around food. Months after my dad's first stroke, his world became a bizarre carousel of snack foods, a sort of regression to his anchovy sandwich days. There was the orange sherbet that he asked for by the gallon, sweet and citrusy, with a pale color the hue of summer clothes. He ate three-bean salad by the jarful, and when he would unscrew the lid of the jar with a pop, the syrupy odor of vinegar was so strong that I could only imagine what the flavor was. My dad would consume that marinated trio with such gusto, the only thing left to do was laugh. And each evening, just before dinner, my mom would call him to the kitchen to get his drink. Trodding to the refrigerator, he would gather bottles of flavored sparkling water. Like an expert mixologist, he would pour a bit of orange, a modicum of unflavored, and a splash of berry. Stirring them all together, he would take a sip, then smack his lips, sighing with contented recognition. The Michael Handler Dinnertime Special.

I AM MY father's daughter; there is a certain irony that we both ended up at Vallejo, with doctors in common. But there was a large part of me that was embarrassed by this common ground. Having a parent who suffers a stroke is an astounding loss, but when you yourself suffer a stroke, well, that is just pitiful. For the first year post-AVM, I was far worse off than my father emotionally. Negotiating the land mines of social situations, deciding how much I wanted to tell people about what had happened to me was intricate. My father, in contrast, would make it his business to tell everyone, the best that he could muster, what had happened to me. We would be out socially and my ears would prick into alertness as I would hear my dad speaking about his youngest daughter who also suffered a stroke. Relative strangers would gasp, my father would nod, and I would fume.

I'm not sure who I thought I was kidding; as I stood with my right arm at a permanent ninety-degree angle, of course there was something wrong with me. But my disability was mine alone to talk about and to inhabit. I thought I was the only person it affected. Little did I know it affected everyone around me in different ways. There was my sister, who thought, Why Adrienne and not me; my mother, who felt the pain of having two people she loved dearly suffer a loss; Brian, who now had a girlfriend with a disability; and my father, though not completely understanding what had happened, who saw a kindred spirit. I think that for my dad there was a slight sense of relief to know that he was not the only one to struggle. For so many years, he had been the uncomfortable center of attention, and now there was someone else to share the limelight. If I would have actually listened, I would have heard him claiming my disability with a sense of pride, even if I wasn't there yet. As my dad so often struggled in finding words to adequately express himself, he often told and retold stories with which he grew comfortable. My story quickly made it onto the roster. But as my father found pride in all that I had overcome, for me, it was an outing. I felt naked and alone.

I would become angry, behaving like a spoiled child, and reprimand my dad for telling people about my secret. But was my disability truly a secret? I felt like the entire right side of my body was painted in neon and I had giant arrows pointing to parts that were not up to par. But I would rather leave people wondering. I was becoming like David and didn't want my disability to be the topic of conversation. My dad's comments seemed to pry open the door for anyone to have a very private discussion about my new disability. He would apologize and I would stew, telling him it wasn't any of his business. He had no right to discuss me. But that was an unreasonable demand. What do you talk about if not your family, friends, work, and playtime? During his apologies and my explanations, my dad would nod sympathetically, agreeing to keep my issues to himself. But the very next time we were together in a social setting, my ears would burn as I would hear my father say, "Yes, a stroke. I know, I know. . . . It's amazing."

GROWING UP, PIE in the Sky was my playground of sorts. I took my afternoon naps on a cot in a darkened warehouse corner. My after-school companions were artists. I would crawl up on the long, ink-splattered tables lined with paint and patterns, watching as they ran massive rolls of masking tape in straight lines, prepping the latest blimp for a soft drink logo. For my sixth birthday, I was given a gift from my parents that I desperately wanted, a Cabbage Patch Kid Preemie, its bald head smooth and tan, like a russet potato. But it was the wrapping of the box, done by one of the artists at Pie in the Sky, that was truly special. Plain white paper was decorated with the most gaudy and magnificent hand-painted birthday cake. It was as if this artist had climbed into my head, sensing the type of birthday cake a preadolescent girl would desire: a pink layered confection, like a wedding cake, minus the rigid bride and groom figurines. It had sugary rosettes and dripping latticework swags, and even though I loved that doll, dragging it around with me for months, it was the wrapping paper, the perfect depiction of the joy of a child's birthday celebration, that I kept folded neatly in my closet for many years.

Now those same tables I sat upon eating my after-school snack and blabbing absentmindedly to the artists became runways on which I practiced my gait. After the workday was through, I would carefully climb up onto the tables, and like Jimmy Stewart in *Vertigo*, I never looked down. Breathing deeply, I would slowly start to walk, unnaturally thinking of each step before I took it. The length of the table stretched before me like a deserted highway. The first few steps were always a miserable collection of stories of a girl, still uncomfortable in her skin and learning to stand on her own again. My mother claimed that this was the only place where she could look up at my spindly legs unobstructed. She would watch me walk and call out commands. "Relax," she would say. "Remember what they told you in Vallejo. You're throwing your hips." There was an edge in her voice that always irritated me. I would roll my eyes as I turned in a huff. This was not the runway of my dreams. My mother would graciously ignore the eye roll, and I would continue my stroll as nonchalantly as I could while on display. "Try not to think so much. I can read it on your face."

In the months following Vallejo, my mother acted as a nurturing parent, but she had also become my physical therapist—one whom I resented for all of her able-bodied ease and respected for her watchful eye. This relationship proved contentious at times. There were moments when I wanted her to simply be mom, the

warm, loving, funny person I knew her to be, but this was someone she could not be. My mother was pushing me, buoying me up.
She was readying me for the outside world. Some parents try to
make their children stand out so that the world can see their importance. But my mother would try, for the first time in her life, to
help me fit in, knowing that this was all I wanted.

"CAN YOU BELIEVE this?" I asked, grabbing yet another dish
from the neat stack in the kitchen cabinet and wrapping it in
newspaper. The paper surrounded the plate like layers of paint,
thick and messy. It seemed as though we had been moving for
months, packing up one life only to unearth it miles away and
begin anew. "I know we're not moving far, but you will love
Berkeley. It has a whole different flavor to it. It's a good place to
start over," I said, thinking of all of the places I would take my
mom, now that we all were moving to the East Bay. Berkeley
Bowl could become her market, too. She could marvel at the
piles of fragrant produce for sale at Monterey Market. We would
drive up University Avenue, past the Indian chaat houses and sari
emporiums, and into the Gourmet Ghetto. I looked over at my
mom, opening up yet another kitchen drawer and rifling through
it. "Does it make you sad at all?"

"Sad? No. Anxious, unsure, of course. But I'm ready. I think
this move is exactly what we all need."

Pie in the Sky had become the PITS. What had once been a
brief acronym had now become a demonstrative word, describing
how everyone involved felt about the once thriving family
business. It was ultimately my mother and my sister who decided
to close shop. After my AVM, I don't think that my mom could

handle the business anymore. The constant pull she felt about having one child who needed her and a husband who symbolized both loss and love was too much. So the two women who had been running PITS decided to close it down. My mother took a much deserved retirement and sold the house that my sister and I had grown up in. She had had enough of her life on the peninsula. The East Bay had been such a place of growth and nurturing welcome for me, and she wanted that reinvigoration, too. Our lives had become stagnant, like a murky pond that had bogged us down with doctors' appointments, therapists, and sickness. Four-pronged canes prodded us and jabbed us from all sides. It was time to gain a new perspective, to start all over again. As my mom and I stood in the kitchen together, as we had done so many times before while keeping an eye on dinner, this time we were wrapping and packing up. I felt the excitement, too.

Some people call it downsizing, but my parents' new house in Oakland was not downsizing; it was right-sizing. This little house was near its neighbors, a novel idea compared to the rambling house of my youth. It was within walking distance of three grocery stores and one of the best bakeries in the East Bay, with its flaky layers of buttery puffed pastry. A stone's throw from a butcher shop where you could order any piece of meat you desired, the shingled gray-and-blue house, with a camellia bush spilling its petals along the kitchen window, and a fragrant, knotty lemon tree in the side yard, offered a new way of life for my mother. It was also five minutes away from Brian and my new apartment in Berkeley.

CHAPTER 10

German-Style Potato Salad
with Asparagus

Spring means barbecues, and barbecues mean potato salad. I am not much for mayonnaise-based dressings. What can I say? I'm a Jew.

Made with crumbled bacon, fresh dill, and asparagus spears, this potato salad is tangy rather than sweet and has more of a vinaigrette dressing. I made it as part of a dinner with good friends one fateful evening. Who knew what would come out of a little potato salad?

1½ pounds new potatoes, quartered or cut into bite-size pieces
salt and pepper to taste
1½ pounds asparagus (16–20 stalks), trimmed and cut into 1-inch pieces
4 slices bacon

1 cup sliced shallots
1 cup chicken or vegetable stock
3 tablespoons Dijon mustard
1 tablespoon white wine vinegar
¼ cup minced fresh dill

Place the potatoes in a saucepan, cover with cold water, and bring to a boil. Salt the water, and continue cooking until the potatoes are tender yet still firm, 15–20 minutes. Drain well and put in a large bowl to cool slightly. Blanch the asparagus by boiling in salted water until crisp and tender. Drain well and add to the potatoes.

In a large skillet, fry the bacon. When crispy, remove it from the pan and crumble into smaller pieces over the potatoes and asparagus. Pour out all but 2 tablespoons of the grease. In the same skillet, sauté the shallots until they begin to brown and season with salt and pepper. Pour in the chicken or vegetable stock and bring to a simmer. Whisk the Dijon mustard into the stock. The sauce will thicken slightly and become murky. Add the vinegar and the dill.

Pour the sauce over the potatoes and asparagus and toss well to combine. Some of the sauce will pool at the bottom of the bowl but will be absorbed shortly by mixing the salad every so often. Taste for seasoning and serve.

serves 6–8

Food for Thought

Remember when you used to kick me out of your house?" Brian asked as he pushed me around on a flatbed cart through the cavernous warehouse of the local IKEA. It was still too rambling of a store for me to hobble around completely unassisted, so this improvised wheelchair would have to do.

I chuckled at the thought. We had been dating for about six months and I was living by myself in a great 1920s apartment that was badly in need of an exterior paint job. Certain sides were celadon green, others primer white or a steely gray. It was as if the crazy landlady had given up when she tried to paint it, surmising it was too formidable a task. But inside, my apartment was cozy and quaint, with a built-in breakfast nook and black-and-white checkerboard tiles on the kitchen floor.

I had always been steadfastly independent—some, like Brian, might even say to a fault. Often, when we had spent what I thought was too much time together, I would kick him out. It wasn't that what he was doing was irritating to me; usually he was quiet, reading a book or doing the crossword, or maybe even watching TV. But I had had enough. "Okay, that's it. It's time for you to go," I would say, as if I were brushing my hands clean after a particularly dirty day of working in the garden. I needed time by myself to do nothing in particular. At first, Brian was offended by these outbursts, but as time progressed, he came to expect them. As I would shut the door behind him, I would enjoy the nothingness that his absence created.

Now, as I watched Brian struggle with box after box of his, or rather our, collapsed, pressed fiberboard bookshelves, I realized that I couldn't kick him out anymore.

NOT LONG AFTER my stay in Vallejo, I had stood downstairs near another curb. Heavily weighted on my new third leg—the four-pronged cane—I watched as boxes slowly emerged from the tie-dyed apartment building. My loved ones became an assembly line of worker ants, each hauling my belongings from one home to another. I noticed my mother's messy cursive penmanship scrawled across one of the boxes: "A's Office." *Office? Did I even have an office? What did I do in this office?* I had no idea. Planning what I would do any farther ahead than next week seemed like too hard a task.

"Okay, I think we have everything," my mother said, giving the rolling door of the moving truck a closing tug. "Do you want to go upstairs and give your apartment a final look?"

A final look? That seemed rather somber, but I did want to say good-bye to my little apartment in Berkeley. It was one of two on the second floor of the building. That meant stairs. My mom followed behind me as I made my way upward, my legs heavily weighted, one step at a time, my left foot meeting my right. I was unsteady and slow, but who's to know if I was putting off the inevitable lonely sight of my hollow apartment. As I opened the front door, I was taken aback by the stark vacancy of my once-home. It was bright and sunny, and now without furniture clogging the flow, it looked so much larger then I remembered.

I hobbled around from room to room making a soundtrack in three beats—foot, foot, cane; foot, foot, cane. Standing in the kitchen, the black-and-white tiles littered with debris from the move, I shook my head back and forth. This felt so final—the end of my college career, and what was I moving on to? Was I really ready for phase two of my life and my recovery? Only time would tell.

Now Brian and I were making a home together, a place where we would hold many dinner parties, where I would do my first cooking for my catering company and devise the first recipes for my cookbook. It would also become the place that would be littered with Therabands for stretching; tennis balls, the perfect size to grasp in my clenched right fist; and silverware with large rubberized handles for me to practice eating with my right hand.

Moving in with your boyfriend postgraduation had always seemed a bit ridiculous to me. I had friends who did it, but many of these relationships ultimately failed, and the girls moved on to living with their next boyfriend, and so on. It was like they were trying on new shoes. If the heel was too tight, they moved on to the next one, which hopefully had a little more room. But ideas change. Brian and I moved in together because, yes, we loved each other and our relationship had withstood so much in its infancy, but also as a way for me to begin to regain my independence. Call me a hypocrite, but here I was moving in with my boyfriend. And we hadn't even *talked* about getting married yet.

We drove back to our empty apartment and parked the car as close to the entrance as we could so that Brian wouldn't have to carry the boxes of bookshelves too far unassisted. I opened the wooden front gate. I was making mental notes of what supplies we still needed to pick up at the local hardware store: hooks for my aprons and nails to hang pictures. I could already imagine the front garden, with a small patio, just large enough for a table and chairs, and a barbecue; it immediately felt like home.

The paint gently peeling off the building was a dusty blue. It was an old 1907 firehouse that had since been converted into apartments by two architects living upstairs—and no, the pole sadly did not remain. To me the house simply looked old and loved, like a favorite chair from the family room in your parents' house that hasn't been touched since the seventies. In the front yard, scented geraniums mixed with sturdy succulents. Vines of star jasmine grew up and over the wooden fence into the neighbor's yard. The place was overgrown and weedy with uncut grass up to my kneecaps. The architects were lazy, tired of maintaining a property that once held so much promise. But to me, it was perfect, an oasis of calm in an otherwise bustling city.

Opening the front door to the apartment, I let Brian stagger in ahead of me. As he made several trips to the car and back, I surveyed our new living area. It was a loft space, with two small bedrooms, and my favorite, the original claw-foot bathtub in the bathroom. Each time I took a bath, sudsing up, I would imagine the firemen peeling off their work clothes and stepping carefully into steaming bathwater. The back wall of the apartment held the kitchen, with plenty of cabinet space to store the dishes, a fair amount of counter space for chopping, and what would quickly become my most prized appliance—the dishwasher.

The living space of the apartment was a palette, with white walls, a high ceiling, and light wood floors. We would eventually fill it with my grandmother's 1930s-era dining room table placed close to the front door. Upon adding a sofa, piano, and some bookshelves, it would become a living room, where we would gather with friends and eventually get married. My desk sat near the front windows, overlooking the garden, covered by stacks of papers, cups of pencils, and my computer; it became a place I would sit for many hours thinking and writing about the food I created in that beloved kitchen.

"THIS IS GREAT," Brian remarked.

"Well, thanks, but you did a fair amount of the chopping. It was a joint effort." Brian and I had worked out an informal system. He would chop the unwieldy vegetables—the onions, the garlic, maybe the last bit of wobbly potato—anything that required a steady hand, not a clumsy stump. And it so happened that most of the vegetables I was unable to cut were the tear-inducing, smelly ones. Perhaps there was something to this disability.

"These tomatoes are great—really flavorful." It was coming to the end of tomato season. The price of heirloom tomatoes was steadily rising as the farmers had fewer to pick and bring to market, so I had purchased mainly Romas, the workhorse of Italian cooking. I had roasted them slowly in the oven. They shriveled and lost their plumpness, yet remained pungent, still tasting of summer. Sautéed with some evenly diced onions, thanks to Brian, and added to the slithery pasta with freshly torn basil—it really was the quintessential late summer pasta dish. "How come the entire dish is tinted pink?" Brian asked.

"In addition to roasting the little Roma tomatoes, I bought one giant beefsteak and grated that raw into the pasta at the last moment."

Grating had become my latest accomplishment. My right hand still remained a clenched fist, but like a mussel shell waiting to be steamed open, I could now open it manually with my left hand. Placing the handle of the grater in my newly opened fist, I could then grasp and grate away. This new method opened a world of mundane activities to me. I now took pleasure in washing dishes, placing dirty utensils in my stump of a right hand, only to suds them clean with my left. I grasped the handles of shopping bags with gusto. To me, the unremarkable truly became remarkable.

"Mmm," Brian slurped. "Well, it's delicious. Where'd you get the recipe?" he asked, eyeing my ever-growing collection of cookbooks.

"I just made it up."

I'M NOT SURE what caused it—maybe it was that I had a small patio of my own, maybe it was that I truly had an interest in preparing and consuming seasonal meals, but Brian and I cooked many meals outdoors. Barbecuing at our house required hunkering down over a miniscule hibachi bought at the local drugstore for under twenty dollars. This hibachi in turn had to be replaced each year because of rust and general wear and tear. From spring to fall, I put it to good use, grilling up sausages accented with fennel seed, and whole butterflied chickens that I splayed out on the grill and squeezed with lemon. Clams were cooked in their firmly closed shells, only to open in minutes from the heat and smoke; and pizzas were done on the grill, with crusts charred and cheese bubbly and brown. We were living the California indoor-outdoor lifestyle.

That first summer in our apartment, we would have our friends Lucy and Frank over for a barbecue every weekend, weather permitting. They would come over for a lazy afternoon lunch or a late-night supper. We would laugh about the latest goings-on at the university; Lucy would complain about roommate woes, or Frank would regale us with his latest escapades in the art department.

"Dinner was great; it's always great," Lucy remarked one evening as she helped me clear the dishes. I must admit, I loved the compliments. On a daily basis, I listened to criticisms in the form of helpful nudging. There were comments about my gait from therapists, about not using my hand and arm in the correct way from my mother, about my inability to behave in the same manner that everyone else does from me—but in the kitchen, there was no criticism. Sure, not everything that I made tasted terrific; I had cakes that fell and sauces that curdled, but they were still *my* creations to tweak. No one else was tweaking me in the kitchen. "Have you ever thought of teaching a cooking class?" Lucy asked.

"Who would want to take a cooking class from me? I have zero formal training in that field. I think you have to get your start somewhere in order to teach, either go to cooking school yourself, or cook in a restaurant, or whatever. I don't think anyone would take me seriously as a teacher; they would all be too enthralled watching me limp around."

Lucy rolled her eyes. "You swear your disability is that noticeable, Adrienne." I could never gauge from people's reactions if they indeed saw me as a disabled person. The girl with the limp arm and the tired foot. There were some people who didn't seem to notice at all. Perhaps they were too self-absorbed or they were really good at hiding their fascination. Others would pointedly stare at me hobbling by them, trying to figure out if I had sprained my ankle or broken my foot. "But whatever, I'm just saying, you should do something more with food rather than cook us all a meal every week. Not that we're not thrilled to be on the receiving end." Lucy picked at the remains of the potato salad in its serving bowl. "I really liked how this potato salad wasn't all mayonnaisey."

"I know. I can't stand a potato salad that's hiding behind globs of sweet-smelling mayonnaise. It grosses me out. That's why I started making this potato salad. It's more like the German sort, but with bacon. Because everything is better with bacon."

"Adrienne!" Lucy exclaimed, interrupting yet another one of my food rants. "You should write a cookbook! That's it! The perfect way for you to get more involved with food—it's obviously what you love. Frank, Brian," she said excitedly to the guys. "Don't you think Adrienne should write a cookbook? I would totally buy it, and I'd get all of my lame-ass friends in the philosophy department to buy it, too. I'd tell them it was a categorical imperative."

"But what do I know about cooking? I mean obviously I know

how to plan and make a meal, but is that enough?" I asked these questions, but my mind was already racing. *Could I really write a cookbook? Maybe I could.*

"You know more than most," Frank remarked.

"I think that's a great idea. Of course, you know how to cook. Our friends are always asking you for recipes; you are never more excited than when you pick up some new item at the market, and you yourself own a ton of cookbooks," Brian said, gesturing to the stacks of glossy food-splattered copies lined up on the kitchen counter. "This is what you're passionate about, isn't it? You should do it. What do you have to lose?"

By the end of the evening, the four of us had polished off another bottle of wine, had another helping of dessert, chattered on about titles and themes of cookbooks, and still I had to be convinced. But the idea was exciting. This seemed to be exactly what I needed in my life. Up until this point, I had become self-obsessed and self-conscious. I didn't make a move without thinking of how my body reacted to the motion. A step was never taken without thinking of how my right foot would land in relation to my left. My mind was continually split. Brian and I would go for evening strolls around the neighborhood, where he would prattle on about his day, and I would listen and nod accordingly but be consumed with whether the step I had just taken was too large or how my right arm was creeping upward, not remaining relaxed at my side. I needed a life outside of therapy. Maybe I could do just that with food and writing.

I willingly became obsessed with food, just as my father had become preoccupied with three-bean salad. I bought a composition notebook—very official. I was ready to begin choosing my recipes. For those first weeks, that notebook was an omnipresent appendage. It had scrawlings and reminders of dishes I had prepared, flavors that were intriguing to me. When I went out to eat, I noticed which foods were often paired together on menus and which were successful combinations. I would get lost in my gastronomical head, reviewing my budding list of recipes, deciding I needed starchy dishes, and then thinking endlessly about potatoes and grains until new recipes sprouted.

Food became more than a pastime; it became a purpose. I had been searching for that intangible something to fill my time and my head. Food became that filler. I made something each day, whether it was my morning toast or that bowl of summery pasta, and I took pleasure in these daily activities. I became bolder in my culinary decisions; and the people around me could see my passion, just as they were seeing their waistbands expanding. Sometimes you just need that nudge.

CHAPTER 11

Rice Pilaf with Mushrooms, Celery, and Onions

Rice is one of those wholesome dishes that is completely settling to me. As an antidote to soothe an upset stomach, my father's mother made him steamed white rice with a pat of butter, sprinkled with cinnamon-sugar. And my dad made the same dish for me when I was growing up. When we would have rice for dinner, my dad would always reserve a portion, and make this sort of pudding for my dessert. I'm not sure if it was the rice, or eating something that had been made especially for me, but cinnamon-sugar rice always made me feel better, no matter what kind of day I had.

It's no coincidence that this rice pilaf is the food that started me off writing my cookbook.

1 tablespoon olive oil
1 tablespoon unsalted butter
1 medium onion, diced
1½ cups thinly sliced cremini
    mushrooms
1 cup diced celery

1 cup long-grain white rice
salt and pepper to taste
1¾ cups chicken or vegetable
    broth
Parmesan cheese (optional)

In a large skillet, heat the olive oil and butter on high until butter stops foaming and oil is very hot. Add the onions, mushrooms, and celery and sauté until decreased in volume by half and the onions become translucent, about 5 minutes. Add the rice and continue to sauté until the rice is completely coated in the oil and butter. Season with salt and pepper.

Add the broth, bring to a boil, cover the skillet, and reduce the heat to low. Continue cooking, covered, for 15 minutes. Remove the lid, stir the rice, and taste for seasoning and for doneness of the rice. If the rice needs more time, cover again and continue cooking for an additional 5 minutes.

Remove from the heat. Sprinkle with Parmesan cheese if desired and serve.

serves 4–6

Too Many Cooks
in the Kitchen

It feels like a giant vat of pee," I complained to my sister as she picked me up one crisp autumn afternoon from my water aerobics class at the therapeutic pool. "It's like those kiddy pools that are always a good ten degrees warmer than the adult pool. No one says anything about it, but you know the reason they get so warm has little to do with the temperature of the chlorinated water and more to do with the fact that kids are swimming around in their own urine."

"But these are old people, Adrienne. Chances are they're not relieving themselves in the pool," Jennifer replied in an attempt to reassure me as she drove me home.

"I know, I know. That's not what I'm saying. It's just that there's something really . . . unsavory about swimming around in a pool that's ninety-five degrees. It's too warm. And don't even get me started on the people." I sat back in my seat, trying to relax, resting my bag with my wet oh-so-flattering Speedo on the floor of the car.

Growing up, we had an unheated, icy swimming pool in our backyard. I would wait all summer for those rare days, the summation of a heat spell, when the pool would actually creep above seventy-five degrees, to dive into the clear aquamarine water toward the garish image of a swordfish that was a mosaic on the bottom of the pool. Even after those days of warm weather when the pool was still chilly, I would have a brief swim and climb from the frigid water after twenty minutes to lie on the warm pavement and dry off, the imprint of my wet one-piece leaving a clear outline on the cement. I guess due to a timid amount of sun, even in the summertime, you really couldn't swim in an unheated pool in the Bay Area, unless of course you were a member of the Polar Bear Swimming Club. This was *not* the case at the Bing Crosby Adult Swim Center, where the air smelled thick of chlorine and the unofficial motto of the indoor pool was the warmer the water, the better.

Over a year had passed posthemorrhage, and in an effort to stay motivated in my rehabilitation, I signed up for every form of physical therapy that seemed remotely interesting to me. There was traditional physical therapy in Vallejo; tai chi classes taught by a soft-spoken fusion jazz guitarist in Berkeley; yoga classes in San Francisco taught by an overly serious practitioner in tiny shorts; dance classes with my teacher from UC Berkeley, which proved to be more of a frustration than a release; acupuncture sessions in Orinda, where I was poked with electrified needles and asked to show my tongue every five minutes; and *now* there were these water aerobic classes. I crisscrossed the Bay Area looking for the one person who had the answer, but something told me it would not be Annie at the Bing Crosby Adult Swim Center.

Like a throwback to my time in Vallejo, I was the youngest participant in my water aerobics class—by a long shot. As I found my way to the locker room, I passed women with walkers; catatonic men in wheelchairs being pushed by disinterested caregivers; and a handful of vital older women who came for the gossip. Each week, I trudged into the women's locker room, careful to avert my eyes from the handfuls of naked older women, their skin soft as leather and their breasts flopping down at their waists. At the age of twenty-two, I wasn't even comfortable enough with my own nubile yet transformed body, let alone the aged bodies of my senior classmates, to brazenly raise my head and look around the locker room. I huddled in the corner of the room to slip into my kelly green racer-back swimsuit.

With the swimsuit poised at my ankles, ready to be pulled up, I glanced at my figure in the full-length mirror. I didn't even recognize the person gazing back at me. Who was this person with these quickly atrophying limbs? My right arm lay limp like the damp pool towels thrown in a heap next to me. My right calf, once solid from hours *en pointe* at the ballet barre, was slowly dwindling in size. I poked the layer of fat insulating my midsection. What was this flabby band coating my belly button? The right side of my back winged out like an angular hood ornament of a fifties automobile. I was not happy with what I saw and quickly bent down to retrieve my swimsuit—at least it sucked in all of my bits and bobs and loose pieces of flesh. Grabbing my towel, I messily wrapped it around myself and stepped out into the steaming hot pool area. The smell of chlorine was intoxicating and reminded me of a German-style spa I used to go to with my family in the wine country. The pool was mostly empty, save for a few slow-moving swimmers floating on their backs. I sat at the edge of the water, sizing up my fellow participants.

One gentleman was wheeled into the pool on a ramp, and once in the water his strategically placed flotation devices took over, keeping him afloat in the pool for the duration of the class. There was also a woman whose disabilities seemed similar to my own. The entire left side of her body hung limp, her shoulder slumped, and her arm lay listless in front of her body. She lumbered along to the edge of the pool, dragging her foot, which acted like the stump of a tree bracing her for balance. In addition to her physical disabilities, Juanita's speech was slurred and she had difficulty remembering what had been taught in the class from week to week. But she seemed enamored with me. In fact, much of the class did.

When I signed myself up for classes taught at a senior center, I knew that questions would soon follow. I was like a precocious child, the Doogie Howser of the disabled community, a role with which I was not comfortable. No elderly person expected someone my age to be suffering from the same maladies that they were. My limp was met with inquisitive eyes, and I stiffly answered the questions about my health or my disability. My answers were met with amazement, followed by kind words of encouragement. "Don't worry, honey; things are going to get better for you." Or, "This is a bump in the road. You'll be back to running around in no time."

Easing myself into the water, I let the warmth surround me.

Class began; I performed a slow-motion aerobic routine, my arms stretched out like the propeller of a mini–prop plane. I followed Annie's motions, stomping in place, forcing the water from underneath my body, only to have it flow back in place. There was nothing aerobic about my routine; I was not fatigued; I did not break a sweat. Instead, I stewed, like a piece of meat braising in that bathwater of a swimming pool.

As I climbed from the pool after class, nodding good-bye and smiling meekly at my senior citizen cohorts, I was getting tired of hearing their admirable statements. I realized their sentiments were only coming from good places, just as the nurses in Vallejo had only kind words, the acupuncturist truly believed she was helping me, and the yogi thought that if I could hold that one pose for a single second longer, everything would be all right. I wanted it to be all right, too, and I wanted this entire ordeal to be over. I was tired of being on the receiving end of positive statements. My life was flashing by so quickly. When I was a child, it seemed that the years were endless. From one birthday to the next seemed an eternity, and waiting each year for the holidays, the benchmarks of time, seemed eons. But now, more than a year had raced by, leaving me hobbling in its wake. I was twenty-two years old and I was tired. This life of constant rehabilitation and scrutiny was not healthy. I needed to feel fulfilled.

Home from the class, I waved good-bye to my sister, the chosen chauffeur of the afternoon, and leaned against the front door to my apartment, dejected. Remembering what my yogi told me, I took a cleansing breath, opened my eyes, and headed into the kitchen. My splattered apron, which had been modified by my mother to include Velcro straps rather than straps requiring a bow to be tied, hung on a hook by the pantry. Donning the apron, I walked to the fridge and stood, staring at its contents the way that people do when they are hungry but nothing looks appealing. We didn't have much—a bunch of celery, an onion or two, a handful of mushrooms. I took them from the fridge and began to prepare them. Washing and slicing the celery, hearing the crunch of the stalks under the weight of the knife, cutting into the mushrooms and watching them oxidize as soon as the moist air of the kitchen hit them, and wiping the tears from my eyes due to the pungency of the Spanish onion as it rolled around on the cutting board, it was all soothing to me, more soothing than any of the therapy sessions I had been to lately.

I chopped and seasoned, sautéed and simmered. Unlike the chemical smell of chlorine at the pool, the smells emanating from the kitchen were real. It was four o'clock in the afternoon, I was not exceptionally hungry, and I was making a rice pilaf, similar to the rice my father used to make for me and his mother used to make for him. It was comfort food. I sat down with a small bowl of pilaf, and with every bite, I was nourished. The overly tepid water in the adult pool was washed away, the encouraging though irritating words of the ladies in swim class were becoming an ignorable din, and the odor of chlorine was covered by the scent of the vegetables that had been sautéed along with the wholesome rice.

I cleared my dishes and sat down at my desk. Opening a new file on my computer, I began to write. I didn't struggle; the prose simply came. The rice had been restorative. The simplicity of the flavor had perked up my tongue, rallied my taste buds, made my fingers dexterous. At last, I turned to the composition notebook that had become an appendage since dinner with Lucy and Frank, and thumbing through the pages, I knew I had something to say. I was writing a cookbook.

NOTHING SAYS MORE about a neighborhood than the types of food that line the shelves at the local market. The grocery store that I grew up with was vast yet standard: plastic gingham bags full of sliced sandwich bread; more than a few boxes of rice mixes with "exotic"-sounding flavors: Mexican Fiesta and Oriental Surprise; heads of iceberg lettuce; and a small selection of boring apples. My new cavernous home of delectable food products was only blocks away from our apartment. Berkeley Bowl was a food lover's dream: part health food store, part ethnic market, part gourmet food shop, with a produce section larger than entire New York City food emporiums. Come summertime, there would be at least three or four types of rosy apricots housed in wooden crates that lined the aisles, not to mention apriums, plumcots, and pluots for those who preferred to mingle their genuses with the delectable plum.

Not every day that I spent toiling over my cookbook was as delightfully simple as the day that I had begun. There were days when my computer sat looming in the corner, the keyboard taunting me and the screen displaying rows of uninspired prose. Each word that I typed seemed trite, every phrase too elementary. I would be blocked, and I knew what I had to do—go to the Bowl for inspiration. Pulling the granny cart behind me, its wheels creaking with each rotation and its wire frame painted periwinkle blue, I would slowly make the sojourn to the market. For once, I would not think about my gait and the length of each stride that I took; instead, I thought about what there would be at this glorious market. What was in season? What perfect piece of fruit would be available? Would there be an herb that I had yet to try? Would I make a protein-filled supper in my sturdy cast-iron dutch oven or would lighter fare be on the menu tonight?

As I approached the final block of my journey, the cars began to pile up around me. People in Berkeley can be vicious when it comes to their organic produce. The same people who gathered weekly at Ashtanga yoga classes, unisex quilting bees, and Tilden Park for lengthy hikes discussing the latest achievements of their precocious honor roll offspring were now honking at one another in their Toyota Priuses, jockeying for a precious parking space in the crowded Berkeley Bowl parking lot. I would slip in the front entrance, thankful for once that I did not have a car.

The chill of the grocery store air gave me goose pimples as the gentle rotting fragrance of ripe fruit filled the air. I would hook the granny cart onto the front of my shopping cart and place my right hand on the handle, letting my palm grasp the bar tightly. Then the obstacle course would begin: bumping carts with people going in opposing directions; swerving to miss the young child running loose among the jars of jam; and having to yell, "Excuse me!" above the conversations of other shoppers who were pausing in the aisles to talk on their cell phones. But I knew that from this strife an amazing meal would be made.

I would take my time, knowing that there really was no such thing as a quick trip to Berkeley Bowl. Multiple heads of cauliflower lay before me like a patchwork blanket of varied hues: chartreuse, purple, orange, and the classic white. Each raised the question: Are you going to take me home? Fragrant Meyer lemons with thin, nubby skins were at home next to Ruby Red grapefruits that tempted me with their rosy glow. Melons stacked as high as I could see, with exotic names and provenances, were practically ready to burst and spew their seeds around the market. I would press delicately and smell carefully, as if each piece of fruit was a prize, each vegetable, nobility.

The smells of the spice aisle would beckon me. Slowly I would peruse the vials, jars, and diminutive bags, grasping a small bag of Mexican oregano, its leaves a dusty green and its fragrance familiar yet somehow different. Tossing it into my overflowing shopping cart, I knew there would be no way that Brian and I could eat all of the contents of this cart by ourselves. My eagerness at the market meant, of course, dinner with friends yet again. And I couldn't be happier. Nothing gave me such joy as feeding my loved ones. As long as Berkeley remained a college town, where people rushed around with philosophy texts and worked late in the art history library, young friends didn't make time to feed themselves properly and would come to eat at our house with eager bellies.

Tick, tick, tick, my mind would slowly begin churning as I approached the fish counter. I would chat with the fishmonger, "What's good?"

"Everything."

"No, really, what's good *today?* There must be some things that are better than others."

And the dance would begin, the to-and-fro between fishmonger and client, the playful banter that exists only between virtual strangers. I would toss my newly purchased mussels, their crisp black shells glinting like obsidian against the utilitarian paper in which they were wrapped, into the cart.

Adrienne Kane

As a rather shy person, I usually keep to myself. But at the market I found myself to be positively verbose. Disregarding unwritten rules of propriety, I peered into other people's shopping carts and asked about the contents. This led to many interesting conversations. I learned that the stinky, spiky fruit was, in fact, the mellifluous durian. I learned that "sour grapes" were not just an idiom but an actual fruit used to add a savory tart element in Turkish cuisine. I learned that inexpensive chicken parts, the nibs from the wings, bits of scaly skin, and the knuckly feet, can make gallons of the most flavorful gelatinous stock. And I was remarkably proud when others asked me the precious question: What are you going to make with *that*? It was validation of my explorations of the market. Others had noticed my careful choices, and they, too, became curious.

CHAPTER 12

Roast Duck with Apples and Sausage

Duck roasted with apples and sausage. The original recipe comes from Julia Child's Mastering the Art of French Cooking, *and when I tried it for the first time, during a dinner party no less, let's just say it left a little to be desired. The flavors in Julia's* Caneton Rôti à l'Alsacienne *were marvelous—the sweet, tart apples and the savory sausage—but my execution of the recipe was a disaster. Never one to leave things be, I have since roasted quite a few ducklings and come up with a less fatty, more mindful recipe. You do have to attend to the duck a bit more than in the original, but the final result is a crisp-skinned, delicious fowl.*

My solution is roasting the entire bird at a high temperature and pricking the skin often. This allows for the duck to exude much of its fat, which can be saved and refrigerated for many weeks. (Duck fat is delicious when used in sautéing potatoes.)

½ pound pork sausage, casing removed, if necessary

4 sweet-tart apples (like Jonathan, Macintosh, Jonah Gold), peeled, cored, and cut into eighths

1 tablespoon sugar

¼ teaspoon cinnamon

2 tablespoons cognac

4 to 5–pound duck

salt and pepper to taste

Preheat the oven to 425°F. In a large skillet, on medium heat, brown the sausage, breaking it into small pieces. Remove from the skillet with a slotted spoon. Cook the apples in the sausage grease, along with the sugar, cinnamon, and cognac, until the apples begin to soften, about 3 minutes.

Season the duck cavity as well as the outside with salt and pepper. Stuff the duck with the cooked stuffing. With a sharp paring knife or carving fork, puncture the duck's skin thirty or forty times all over—breast, back side, legs, and so on. Place a rack in a large baking dish and sit the duck, breast side up, to roast in the oven.

After 15 minutes, remove the duck from the oven and prick all over again. Continue this process every 15 minutes for 1 hour total. The duck is cooked to medium when juices from the fattest part of the thigh run faintly pink and an instant-read thermometer reads 180°F. If you like your duck slightly more well done, roast for an additional 10 minutes.

Remove from the oven, tent with foil, and let cool slightly before carving.

serves 4

Party Food

I've been thinking, do you want to get married?"

I wasn't completely surprised by Brian's proposal; but I was taken aback. Since we had moved in together, Brian and I had spoken about marriage in the abstract. We were going to be married . . . eventually. It was inevitable; it was only a matter of when. Brian made me laugh and comforted me when I was a bundle of nerves. He helped me in the kitchen as we chatted about the day's events, his grad school woes, and my latest foibles in therapy. We knew each other better than anyone else and I loved him dearly. But even after three years of dating, and now, two years of living together, I was still a little bit stunned.

"Wait, what? Do I want to get married? To you? Now?" I practically fell off the bar stool at the Spanish tapas place where Brian and I were dining. Sitting up a bit straighter, I looked right at him, trying to read his body language.

"Well, yes, to me; and yes, right now. I've been thinking, we've dated long enough. I'm finishing up school; you have this enormous undertaking of the cookbook. Things are going to be happening for both of us—I have a good feeling," he said relaxed, then took a sip from his Pisco Canary. I was shocked by all of Brian's rosy optimism. Where was the Jewish pessimist I had grown to love? "I'm just saying, we don't know what the future holds for either of us, but I can't imagine you not being a part of my life."

I took a moment to register all that Brian had said. Then I calmly said, "Okay."

"Okay?"

"Yeah, okay."

And then he did the most romantic thing of all. He put out his left hand. He wanted to shake on it, on our engagement. And to me, that was perfect. People shake hands when they enter business deals, when they close escrow on their very first house, possibly even when they are buying a new car. Why not shake on a marriage proposal? *That* is a very adult decision. Brian and I were truly entering into a life together. Years ago, I tried to send him packing, and now, Brian was in this for the long haul.

Six weeks later, we were married. We had toyed with the idea of eloping to Las Vegas but ultimately decided to get married in the living room of our apartment in Berkeley, surrounded by a select few. Maia flew out from law school in New York with her boyfriend, Gabe, and a few friends who seemed to have been there from the beginning gathered in our apartment on a Sunday afternoon. Our parents huddled together on our living room sofa; Brian's sister, always emotional, blotted her tears; and my sister, teetering on a pair of bright pink faux alligator pumps, gripped the arm of her husband. They all watched as we took our vows in front of Lucy and Frank, who had gotten ordained for the occasion on the Internet.

The morning of our wedding, I awoke, lying next to my husband-to-be in our bed, which was much too petite for two people, and never once second-guessing, I knew that he was my ideal. Whatever happened from this point on, we would always be bound together, and I was ready to be linked to this person. "Bri, get up. We have a big day ahead," I said, nudging him awake. My stomach gurgled, and I wasn't sure if the churning came from hunger pains or my nervous excitement. Grabbing a piece of toast and pouring an inky cup of coffee, we were off to the bakery to pick up our cake.

A short walk from our apartment was Crixa, a sunny Hungarian pastry shop with dour ladies guarding the refrigerated cases that housed rows of delectable sweets. I had been faithfully going to this bakery since my first summer back in Berkeley. Strolling by, a rhubarb-apricot pie beckoned to me, its crust so buttery it was ethereal, melting on your tongue and mingling with the fragrant fruit. I never quite understood how the women working there could be so serious. Patrons of a bakery are immediately put in an elated mood as they think of the many sweet morsels of food to eat. It didn't seem possible for successful bakery owners to be less than sweet themselves, but for the most part, the women working at Crixa were. Maybe it was a test. If you could put up with the moods of the owners, you would be sweetly rewarded. After a while, though, the moods made no difference to me, and one of the owners even cracked a smile when I asked her to create our wedding cake.

The bakery didn't bake traditional wedding cakes, which was fine for our nontraditional wedding. I asked for one of my favorites, the Stefania Cake—a towering layer cake of vanilla genoise sandwiched between smooth milk chocolate buttercream and frosted entirely in this same rich buttercream. This cake is perfect and simple. Although it may sound like it is too decadent, too sweet, it is the apotheosis of dessert. Picking up the cake, I excitedly thanked the somber chefs and got back into the passenger seat of the car, readying my lap to transport the tower of chocolate buttercream to the restaurant. I would have to wait to enjoy it, though—there was a wedding and a dinner that I would have to get through first.

We hurried back to our apartment just in time to meet the florist, who was unloading boutonnieres and bouquets from the back of her van. Tucked underneath a damp cloth was my bridal bouquet. I had asked the florist to incorporate fruits or vegetables in the arrangement, but I had no idea what she would concoct. Lifting the cloth, she revealed a bouquet that was exotic for January in California. With ruffled peonies and spidery orchids, its focal point was a deep purple artichoke. It was the perfect bouquet for a bride with a growing love for food.

Brian looked dapper in his new pinstripe suit and I wore a festive gray dress. As weddings go, our ceremony was over quickly, ending with a rock out to Tom Jones's "It's Not Unusual." And everyone joined us for an intimate meal at Downtown restaurant. It was winter, the sky darkened early, and the previous night's rain still collected in shallow puddles on the sidewalk. The craggy brick walls of the restaurant offered a welcoming warmth as we all took our seats around one long table. Rousing toasts and sentimental tears of well-wishers punctuated the evening's meal, where the food was brought out seamlessly. There were salty olives, each ensconced in a tempura-like batter and fried to a golden crisp. There were platters of rustic and eggy blue cheese tarts, nestled among beds of winter greens, offering a bitter crunch to the polish of the pastry. These starters were followed by seared halibut, which I had selected, knowing Downtown's specialty is seafood. The fish had a buttery finish and was joined by a cauliflower purée so light and creamy that it seemed to only whisper a mention of the hearty vegetable with which it was made. And to top the evening off, the glorious Stefania Cake.

It was the perfect day. Relaxed, intimate, and low stress—I guess it was the way that Brian and I have continued to try to lead our lives. With our loved ones surrounding us, the ceremony signaled a new beginning. My life was becoming complete.

"JULIA DIED."

"What? Who?"

"Julia Child. She died . . . at her home in Santa Barbara," I mumbled in disbelief.

"Well, how old was she? Old, right? She lived a long and full life," Brian said consolingly.

"But you don't understand what a formidable figure in American cooking she was. Julia was the one person who brought cooking to the masses on TV in the sixties, and now there's an entire network dedicated to it. Without her, who knows, we still might be eating peas served from a can."

Everyone in my family loved Julia Child. My uncle was in cooking school when she hit her prime on PBS. Saturday afternoons were spent at my grandma's house watching reruns of *The French Chef.* I was mesmerized as she hoisted her cleaver high above her head then came down on a piece of meat; she was like a construction worker wielding a sledgehammer. For the longest time, I thought that she was English due to her bizarre sing-songy accent. That was until my uncle explained it as a peculiar dialect of American English—Americans with money.

"We should have a party, like a wake, but a commemorative dinner party for her," I decided out loud. "And I will cook all Julia food from *Mastering the Art of French Cooking,* the book that truly started the U.S. food revolution." With that, I began poring over my two-volume set. I had never really cooked from Julia's early books, but it seemed that every serious cook at least owned these volumes—and I was beginning to become a serious cook. It was August when Julia died, though we didn't have the dinner party until mid-October. By the time I had decided on a menu, drawn up the small guest list, and invited those guests, fall had already rolled around. Indian summer had come to a close, and although in California we don't typically have a stunning autumn, the leaves, a riot of burnt colors, were falling swiftly to the ground.

About one week before the party, I got an idea. Each Halloween, my uncle would hold large drag parties, and one year he dressed as the formidable Mrs. Child, wearing a garish elastic-bottomed shirt. I decided that at this dinner party our guests would have to don similarly styled elasticized shirts. They would sip cool vichyssoise while nestled snuggly in their culinary grandam-themed outfits. I quickly told Brian of my latest plan, and we hopped in the car, heading to the local thrift store.

Old ladies must be dressing better nowadays. The last time I had frequented a thrift store, I was an alienated youth listening to Cream and toting around a copy of Kerouac's *On the Road* as I shopped for boys' blazers that fit tightly in the shoulders and vintage T-shirts. Shopping for dinner party attire, I found the stores to have the same fragrance of mothballs and Jean Naté cologne, although the clothes came with a heftier price tag. It seemed that elasticized waistband shirts were becoming all the rage. Either that, or elderly ladies, with their hair softly tinted blue, realized that these shirts weren't the most flattering of ensembles. It took scouring the Salvation Armies and Goodwills of the East Bay, eventually venturing farther from the university and out into the wilds of Oakland, to find the shirts we were looking for. Some were solid and pastel-colored, others had a bright appliqué of autumnal flowers, and the shining find of the day was reminiscent of a sailor's costume—if sailors wore purple, that is.

The next Saturday, the table was set. Each dining chair was festively adorned with a painstakingly scavenged-for Julia Child–inspired elasticized shirt pulled over the back. On the kitchen counter lay my immersion blender, which moments ago had been hard at work whirring together potatoes and leeks. My first course was simple to make and delicious to eat: vichyssoise. This classic French soup is a typical Julia Child masterpiece; with a handful of ingredients, it tastes clean yet somehow sumptuous. I tasted, smacking my lips together, and seasoned with a bit more salt, knowing that flavors dull when they are chilled, and set the pot in the refrigerator. The soup was a hit. So much of a hit that Jon, the perennial bachelor of the guests, asked for seconds and proceeded to pick up his bowl, draining the final droplets of soup into his open mouth.

On to the main course: *Caneton Rôti à l'Alsacienne,* roast duck with apple and sausage stuffing. There is a certain perennial wisdom about trying new recipes for a dinner party—it can be dicey. Cooks are advised to stick to tried-and-true recipes that are well loved, often prepared, and leave few surprises. But I had never run into problems with new recipes before; and what better way to try new flavors than with a group of eager, friendly eaters, right? Well, in this case, I was wrong. Quite wrong.

Earlier in the day, I sautéed and stuffed the birds. Brian trussed—with some pointers and only minor cursing—and then I roasted. But as my diners were assembled, the final spoonfuls of vichyssoise being gulped, I noticed that the ducks were not roasting according to plan. I consulted—and cursed the recipe's instructions. "How is *this* supposed to teach me how to master anything?" I mumbled. Perhaps the oven wasn't hot enough. Perhaps it was that I doubled the recipe, needing to feed everyone with a duo of stuffed ducks. Perhaps Julia Child did not want me to actually master the art of French cooking. But my ducklings were not lovely and golden brown; they were peaked and smelled of fat. Lots of fat. Enough fat that I spent the better part of my evening siphoning rivulets of fat from my once-quacking duo every fifteen minutes.

After more than an hour of ardently watching my ducks getting cooked, though remaining a buttery, yellow color, I got tired of waiting. I had hungry guests to feed, so I stuck the roasting pan under the broiler. The kitchen erupted in a cloud of smoke from the burning fat, though with help from the broiler, the ducks did acquire the sought-after golden crispness. Sickened with the whole affair, I placed the birds on the cutting board and called

Brian in to carve. This has never been one of his strong suits, and we both devotedly wish that carving could be a one-handed task. He massacred; I in turn beautified the birds, gave the guests a helping of Brussels sprouts braised in butter, which incidentally were undercooked, and then we sat down to eat.

The company was delighted. Some diners even asked for seconds of the duck, which I was more than happy to give—I wanted those greasy birds out of my sight. I should be fair—the meal was not horrible; it was just that I had wanted everything to be perfect. I was a cook; this was what I was supposed to be good at. I was writing a cookbook for god's sake.

For dessert I made a beautiful *crème renversée*, or crème caramel. It plopped out of its mold like a dream, quivering ever so slightly. It tasted pure, of vanilla, and of burnt sugar, as it was supposed to. So the commemorative dinner party had a good first course and a promising close to the meal. Conversation flowed with ease—it was a memorable evening. But after everyone headed home at the end of the night, un-self-consciously still wearing their elasticized shirts, which hid their slightly bloated bellies from an evening of too much classic French food, I closed the front door behind them and announced, "I am *never* having another dinner party." Brian nodded, knowing a hyperbolic utterance when he heard one.

On Tuesday, I was back up at Vallejo. My mom and I had made the drive for my bimonthly outpatient physical therapy session. The first half hour was not so much therapy as it was torture. I lay on a large table several feet off the ground, and in between grunts and groans, Tom, who had been my physical therapist for years, stretched me out. It is amazing how tight a person's body can get.

149

He hovered over my twitching body, facing me and standing at my waist. Grabbing my leg around the calf, Tom would rest it on his shoulder. Then, while pressing on my opposing hip, he would slowly lean forward—all in the name of giving me a good hamstring stretch. Through this all, I was told to "try and relax." Instead, I grimaced. Usually Tom would keep conversation going through these intimate and pain-inducing sessions.

"So, did you have a nice weekend?"

"Yeah, it was good but stressful. You see, Brian and I had this dinner party. A Julia Child commemorative dinner party to be exact."

"Who? Keep your hips planted firmly on the mat." I was used to our conversations being interrupted with instructions.

"You know, Julia Child. Aaahhh, that's my leg, thank you very much!" I retorted. "She was the author of *Mastering the Art of French Cooking* and she had several cooking shows on PBS."

Tom shook his head back and forth. "Never heard of her."

"Okay. . . . Well, she was the grandam of French cooking in America. She died a few months ago, so we had a party commemorating her life in food. I made a bunch of her recipes."

"Sounds fun . . . okay, that's all for the torture; let's work on your gait on the parallel bars now."

And that's when I realized that maybe food wasn't the end-all be-all for everyone. I lived in an isolated community—one where Alice Waters's name was uttered with reverence on an almost daily basis. But there were people, like Tom, and countless others I have encountered since, who only saw food as nourishment. You have to eat to live. But food was becoming more important to me, its nuances and subtleties, its tastes and flavors. Hopefully every person finds her strength, the thing that she loves to do. For Tom, it was inflicting pain through seemingly helpful, assisted stretches; and I was starting to realize that I had found my strength, too, in cooking.

CHAPTER 13

Polenta Squares with Onion Confit and Kalamata Olives

When making polenta, patience is a virtue. But once you give in to time, letting it pass over you slowly as you stand by the stove, you will be deliciously rewarded. A palette on which many flavors can be beautifully added, it can be a side dish, an entrée, porridge, or a patty. Butter yellow in hue, smooth in texture, voluptuous in consistency, it has always seemed incredible to me that a few grains of brittle ground cornmeal can become something so warm and sustaining.

Polenta squares were one of the first recipes that I devised for cocktail party fare, and they were one of my mainstays throughout my years of catering. Each element of the recipe can be made early, then assembled when needed, so I'm not even sure why I was thrown into such a panic while making them for the first time. Call it beginner's luck, but these squares and many other hors d'oeuvres that I made for my very first party became my signature cocktail party dishes.

Adrienne Kane

FOR THE POLENTA:
4–5 cups liquid (one-half
    stock, one-half water;
    or all water; or any
    combination)
I cup polenta, or medium-
    ground cornmeal
I tablespoon olive oil
salt and pepper to taste
2 tablespoons minced fresh
    sage

FOR THE ONION CONFIT:
4 tablespoons unsalted
    butter
4 cups thinly sliced yellow
    onions (⅛ inch thick)
½ cup water
salt and pepper to taste

Bring one-half portion of the liquid to a boil. In a large pot, over medium heat, add the polenta or cornmeal, the other one-half portion of liquid, olive oil, salt, and pepper. Bring to a boil, stirring constantly. The cornmeal should absorb liquid rather quickly. Once the polenta is the consistency of porridge, add in a ladleful of boiling liquid, stirring constantly until absorbed. Turn the heat to simmer to prevent scorching. When the polenta has thickened again, add another ladleful of liquid. Repeat this process until all of the liquid has been used. This should take about 10 minutes.

Continue simmering the polenta over low heat for an additional 15 minutes. Add the sage and cook for 10 minutes more. If at any time the polenta is getting too thick, add ¼ cup of water. Taste for seasoning. The polenta should be well seasoned at this point.

Lightly grease a 9 × 13 inch pan with additional olive oil. Pour the polenta into the pan, spreading evenly. Place the pan of polenta in the refrigerator to cool and set for at least 2 hours. This step can be completed a day in advance.

To make the onion confit, melt the butter in a medium-size cast iron or heavy skillet, over low heat. Add the onions and salt

154

immediately, to begin the sweating process. Cook for 10 minutes, stirring occasionally. You do not want the onions to color; you are only sweating them. Add ¼ cup of water, season with salt and pepper, and continue cooking for 10 minutes more. The onions will begin to color slightly. When the pan is dry, add an additional ¼ cup of water and continue cooking, stirring occasionally, for 10 minutes more. During the final round of cooking, the onions will become caramel colored and sweet; continue cooking for 10 minutes more. The onions can be made and refrigerated one day in advance.

TO ASSEMBLE THE POLENTA SQUARES:
prepared polenta
onion confit
35 pitted kalamata olives

Slice the polenta into small squares by running a knife through five by seven times. The polenta should be firm and release with ease onto a serving platter. Take a teaspoon of confit and mound it in the center of each polenta square. Place one olive on top of the confit on each square. You should have a neat little stack of pungent delicacies to serve your guests.

makes 35 bite-size squares

Catering to You

It's a cocktail party at the Berkeley Art Museum." Brian had proposed the idea casually to me one night over dinner. "You would just be supplying the food; drinks are taken care of. I think the party's for about forty people, but I can double-check. Look, the music department offered the job to you. They haven't even tasted any of your cooking. For all they know, you could be frying up packs of cocktail weenies. They'll be pleasantly surprised with your food. Bryce knows about the cookbook and thought you might like a little catering job. I think you should do it."

"I don't know. Forty people isn't exactly small. What would I cook? If not cocktail weenies, then what?" I asked facetiously.

"That's the least of your problems. You always think of amazing things to make."

"Yeah, but you're my biggest supporter."

"Here's Bryce's number." Brian handed me his boss's card, ignoring my nerves. "I told him you would give him a call. Just find out the specifics. And you know that I will help you in whatever way I can."

The specifics were not very specific. The music department had a strict budget. They were tired of eating the same old wine and cheese buffet after every talk put on by the department, but other than that, everything was up to me. "We want to try something a little different. I mean cheese is great—we love cheese—but there has to be something else, too," Bryce told me over the phone. It wasn't as if I was interviewing for the position to cater this event—which was good, because I wasn't sure what I would say—it was as if I already had the job. The event was in three weeks. That gave me three weeks to decide what would be appropriate cocktail food, three weeks to try out new recipes, three weeks to fret over preparation, and three weeks to work myself into a giant mass of nerves. I had some catering experience—if you can call it that—but that was a long time ago.

It was the summer after sixth grade, and I had discovered *The Baby-sitters Club* book series. I guess it is perfectly understandable that I desired the typical preteen world of riding your bike to the corner store and having friends who lived on your block. But years earlier, my parents moved the family to Hillsborough, a place where there were no corner stores, the streets were windy and hilly, and children, let alone peers, were few and far between. There were rambling, often multilevel homes, set back from the street. To deter strangers from venturing into this strange land, the streets remained dark and looming, without streetlights. Loitering of any kind was so strongly discouraged that there were no neatly lined sidewalks to be had.

Hillsborough's most common inhabitant was the moneyed, arcane matron. So instead of friends with which to create a babysitter's club of my own, I had employers and catering. This wasn't catering in the traditional sense. I would arrive at 350 Tartan Trail on a Saturday afternoon, wearing the requisite black pants and white shirt. Tieing on a half-apron, I would get to work, chopping vegetables, setting the table, whipping cream into billowy peaks for dessert. In the kitchen, at twelve years old, I was the matron's right-hand girl—the girl whose presence would calm the matron's nerves as she rushed around the kitchen preparing for yet another one of her lavish parties. At times, I would help serve the meal, always saying the appropriate "excuse me" and refilling water glasses when requested. My real job, however, was the cleanup. I guess you could have called me a rent-by-the-hour maid. None of my employers or guests at the dinner parties thought it strange that I was so young. My parents let me go to work, thinking that it was valuable that I saw how other people ran their homes. I guess no one really cared about child labor when there was shrimp cocktail to be served.

The Ledbetters were frequent entertainers; therefore, I was frequently paid help at their house for dinner parties. My services had been recommended by a friend's mother who mentioned what backbreaking work her dinner parties were. For as neatly as the meals were presented, Mrs. Ledbetter cooked like a blind man paints a house. She cooked, then adjourned to the dining room, where I would hear the rumbles of conversation and the eruptions of laughter as I stood at the kitchen sink, sponge in hand, propagating mounds of suds, like a vigorous germ of lather, to wash up the stacks of pots and pans. "Dear, be careful with those dishes. They're *very* expensive," Mrs. Ledbetter chirped as she glided in from the dining room.

Connie Ledbetter was an East Coast transplant. She was an expert homemaker, with frosted hair styled in an updo that neither moved nor looked like it had ever been touched. Mr. Ledbetter was a dentist, with pearly whites that glistened like a row of diamonds. The amount of hair he was missing on his head was far made up for by his wife's towering coiffure. Connie threw themed dinner parties. There was the Asian-themed party, where the centerpiece for the table was a mini–Chinese lantern festively mingled with freshly cut cherry blossoms. For her Moroccan-inspired shindig, sheets of opulent jewel-tone fabric surrounded an enormous hookah that was used not for tobacco but to house handfuls of colorful flowers.

"Tonight's dinner party is something I like to call 'Under the Sea,'" Connie proclaimed while painstakingly pushing a stick of butter into a fish-shaped mold to arrange as a spread on each butter plate.

"Okay," I said, wondering if any of the guests would care to know that the butter they were about to slather on their bread had been touched, pressed, and toyed with by their hostess.

"The guests are about to arrive, so let's get the salads together."

Mrs. Ledbetter's salads were as old-fashioned as her living room sectional sofa. Feathery tearings of red leaf lettuce were weighed down by circular slices of snowy white hearts of palm. A scattering of toasted pine nuts—very avant for 1990—were tossed on top. "Adrienne, here are some shrimp that I blackened earlier today. Please place a few on each salad plate. I would like them all to be evenly dispersed," Connie said, wiping her hands off on her soiled apron that was protecting her magenta caftan, before racing to catch the door. The guests were arriving.

As the Ledbetters' friends congregated in the dining room, oohing and aahing over this party's centerpiece—a bulbous glass fishbowl with real goldfish swimming among the stems of floppy flowers—the phone rang. It was the final guest calling to say that she was under the weather and would be unable to make it. Connie burst back into the kitchen. "Adrienne, Ms. Charles won't be attending tonight, so it looks like we have made an extra salad. Feel free to have it." Before I could even say thank you, Connie headed back to her guests. But not before saying, "Just take the shrimp off of your salad and distribute them on the other salad plates. Waste not, want not!"

Is that what my salad would have become, waste from yet another Ledbetter dinner party? I wanted to know how much each of those shrimp cost—that they were too expensive to give to "the help." Talk about cheap—my little twelve-year-old body seethed with anger. I was too young to give Mrs. Ledbetter a pithy remark yet old enough to feel that I had been somehow wronged. That night, I refilled water glasses and cleared salad plates as expected. Counting each fishy shrimp tail left behind, I vowed never to work for the Ledbetters again, all the while plotting my revenge. I was a woman scorned.

Toward the end of the evening, amid the clink of coffee cups returning to their saucers, I stood on a step stool, putting the dinner plates away, and I decided to give the Ledbetters their comeuppance. Picking up the hot plates fresh from the dishwasher to put on the top shelf, I brought each one up to my face. But rather than gaze at my reflection in the sparkling china, I opened my mouth, stuck out my pillowy tongue, and licked the surface of every plate.

I never worked for the Ledbetters again. They called for me, but I always said I had a babysitting job, which sadly I did not. I did learn a few things from the Ledbetters, however: how to turn a plain stick of butter into a stupendous centerpiece, that I didn't really like toasted pine nuts, and how *not* to treat the people who are serving you. In my catering business, I knew that I would never make butter molds unless specifically asked, I knew about personal preferences, and I knew that if my business ever grew to the size where I needed to hire people to help, I would treat them with respect.

COULD I REALLY do this? I guess it was too late to be asking myself this question while up to my elbows in creamy polenta. It was molten, getting more viscous with every stir. My mind raced with every turn of the wooden spoon in the school-bus yellow dutch oven that had affectionately been named "the polenta pot." I never make the instant polenta, although today it has become almost more common on grocery store shelves than the original. Like a slick ten-speed versus a trusty tricycle, it is faster, but the speed forces you to miss out on the quality: the unctuous body, the subtle corn flavor, and the sheer heft of the dish. Pouring the snowflakes of cornmeal into the liquid, you must stir, and stir, then taste, and yes, probably stir some more. But what you will end up with is the ultimate in satisfaction.

I have enjoyed polenta in a variety of ways: loose, as a base for grilled sausage; seasoned with Parmesan cheese and woodsy fresh sage as a side dish; made with milk and nestled under a drizzling of pure maple syrup for a leisurely breakfast; grilled in the summertime; fried in the fall. The list of possibilities is endless. Today, it was polenta squares.

Lining up baguette slices for crostini, I brushed each with a swipe of olive oil. I placed my right hand on the cutting board to steady each fig as I sliced it into quarters. The oven was lit, emitting heat into the airy kitchen as I roasted large platters of winter squash. This was the busywork that I had come to value, but I let my mind spin out of control while I carried on with the day's kitchen activities. There are times when the monotony of the kitchen is soothing. The rustle of vegetables being tossed is settling; the rhythmic jumping of a knife against the cutting board is comforting to my ears. But on this day, the monotony was alarming. This was a graduation day of sorts—a day when I would not be closing the door to my rehabilitation work but opening the door to a new life. My rolling pin and roasting pan would be jockeying for space next to my Therabands and Theratubes. I was clearing space for a life in the kitchen; I only hoped that the response to this event would allow me to do it.

THE BERKELEY ART Museum is a Brutalist structure that you either love or hate. Poured gray concrete is the favored material for everything—floor, walls, exterior—all concrete. Imposing from the outside to be sure, but upon entering I had always found it to be breathtaking in its modern functionality. Deibenkorns hang next to Hoffmans, Calders stand next to Rabinowitch sculptures, and in the front lobby there was to be a buffet table filled with hors d'oeuvres of my making. My polenta squares would be in good company.

Brian and I had gone to the museum the week before the event to scope everything out. "So I don't exactly understand what you're so nervous about?" Brian asked as we took a seat in one of the gallery spaces.

"I don't know. I just am," I said, knowing that if Brian were to push the subject even slightly, I would give. And, of course, he did.

"It will be a success. You know that it will."

I nodded, gazing down at my feet encased in sensible brown shoes. There were times when I would be struggling to shove my foot into one sensible shoe or another, cursing their closed, rounded toes. I used to be a girl who truly loved her shoes. It was instilled in me from the time I was young. My father was not a dapper man. In fact, for many years he wore short-sleeved, elastic-waisted shirts, a bit like Julia Child, which were cringe-worthy to the preteen me. But when he dressed up, donning his camel hair blazer with the gleaming gold buttons, he would always pull out his cordovan dress oxfords from the recesses of the closet. He must have loved the oxblood sheen of those shoes as much as I did.

An hour before my dad dressed to go out, I would find him standing in the laundry room, shoes laid out on the washing machine. Hidden away on a shelf was a little kit—a collection of hockey puck–size shoe polishes, spent rags, and blackened soft brushes with the bristles bent and splayed out in every direction. I would climb up and sit cross-legged on the dryer. The chemical odor of the shoe polish and the whisking noises of the brush filled the room as my dad cleaned off the dust that had settled on his shoes. We would talk, dad showing me tricks to make your shoes sparkle. He taught me to take care of the things I truly loved.

I had had some fantastic shoes. My first slip-ons were a shiny pair of black patent leather shoes with a convertible ankle strap: on for extra support, off when you were feeling particularly daring. I even had a pair of blue suede shoes, navy blue nubuck to be exact, with iridescent leather curlicues at the toes—they looked like avant shoes for a jester. I adored those shoes, squeezing my feet into them long after I had outgrown them. Later there were gray, strappy, high-heeled sandals, with a poof of soft rabbit fur embellishing the toe. With a narrow gravity-defying heel, comfort was not the key, but I did not care. These were a thing of beauty.

Now, staring down at my clunky brown shoes at the Berkeley Art Museum, scuffed from constant stumbling, soles worn unevenly, they told a different story. I wore them not proudly as I had donned my blue suede shoes, but with humility. These were not the shoes of my peers, telling stories of late nights out and mornings spent gulping a cup of coffee before dashing out the door to work. These were the shoes of a decrepit woman who needs comfort, solace, and support.

"It's not the food I'm worried about. Food I can do."

"Then what is it?"

"People. They'll be watching me. You know how I hate to be looked at. I just want to be left alone."

"And who says you won't be? Listen, I've worked tons of catered events as a jazz musician. Let me tell you what I see: People will descend on the food like vultures. Ultimately, they won't care who is serving, how it was prepared, or even how it got there. Give them a shovel. People are self-absorbed. So, let them be self-absorbed; that way, they won't be watching you."

That was Brian, the misanthrope who I loved. I knew that he was right. The disabilities that I suffered were physical, but it was the emotional disabilities—the paralyzing insecurities that followed me through my daily activities—that I continually needed to confront. "I know. You're right. It's going to be fine, right?"

"It will be better than fine. This is a case of nerves," Brian said, getting to his feet. "Do you want to look at the space once more before we get going?"

I nodded, glancing down at my shoes once again. They weren't so bad. They were actually the typical Berkeley woman shoe, functional and sensible, and an entire town of women can't all be wrong, can they?

I HAD RECRUITED my mom and sister to lend a hand in setting up. Diligently we brought plate after plate of food into the gallery space of the museum. As I prepared the fig crostini, slathering the ricotta cheese onto the slices of baguette, I wondered: Would there be enough? What if people turned up their noses at the humble roasted vegetables?

"Don't worry about it. I know what you're thinking," said Jennifer, patting me on the back. "The table looks beautiful; the space couldn't be nicer. Just relax."

I nodded, knowing that what my sister said was true. But ultimately it didn't matter what she thought. In a few moments, the crowd would descend and the noshing would begin. Then

I would know. Would people be polite, choking down the treats made for them by the cripple?

The doors to the gallery were thrown open and people trickled in. For the first moments, they stood, surprised that the spread of food was in fact for them. Slowly, like the first couple entering the dance floor at the junior high school dance, the first few stragglers approached. They perused, deciding which food was the most tempting. Then the attack began. The fig crostini were the first to go—so delectable at their peak of freshness. Another diner attacked the cheese plate, swooping in to take a dig at the creamy Camembert. I peeked around the corner into the gallery and my body went limp with relaxation. The crowd had transformed from a nerdy, cerebral group to ravenous diners surrounding the buffet table.

The fig crostini were decimated. Bits of ricotta cheese that had fallen from the disks of toasted baguette mingled with the verdant chiffonade of fresh basil. Roasted fall root vegetables that had escaped from heaping platters to be deftly dipped into creamy mustard-flavored aioli were lying every which way on top of the starched white tablecloths. There was nothing left of the cheese platters, save for rinds of melting Camembert. A few olives rolled around in their marinating liquid, displaying their muted dresses of green and purple. The mini-jacketed potatoes, once so fresh that their skins shone a toasty brown, were now withered and dried. As for the polenta squares that I had primly sliced into parallelograms that morning, there was not a single one left behind. If what was left of the food was any indication of the party's success, then this was a raging, bombastic hit.

I headed into the gallery to begin the clearing. As I gathered the platters, I felt a tap on my shoulder. Here we go; I had prepared a mini-speech, informing curious guests about why their caterer was disabled. "Are you the caterer?"

I nodded.

"This food was wonderful. Simple and delicious. I'm having a small party next month, and this is exactly the sort of food I love. Would you happen to have a card?"

I blinked. "Of course. I'm so glad you enjoyed it. My cards are in the back; I'll get one for you." I gathered the platters in my left hand, then limped to the back of the gallery, a smile clearly planted on my face for the first time that day.

FROM THAT POINT on, things got easier. The business snowballed: a cocktail party turned into a dinner party, which turned into a baby shower, and a thriving business, Nosheteria Catering, was born. The once-new skin of a disabled young woman was still a battle that needed confronting; and figuring out where I stood in a world that I did not feel completely a part of would take some time. But the catering business gave me some sense of place. More important than having a bit of rent money was having a vocation and another purpose to my life. Now, when I would attend a party and people asked what I did for a living, my career could be succinctly stated, "I'm a caterer." People would nod. Some would ask how I got into it. Others would move on to unspecified question number two. I was able to deflect the emphasis from falling onto me, and this brevity was somehow settling.

CHAPTER 14

Butternut Squash and Green Apple Soup

Make a recipe, blog about it, make a recipe, blog about it. So goes my life.

I never thought I would be a blogger. But I never thought that I would be a caterer, either, and if there is one thing that I have learned from my life, it's that it can't be planned for. Sometimes it is a joy, showing the food that comes out of my kitchen to countless anonymous readers. Sometimes it is a drudgery; I want to eat, not pause to take a photo of the food that I made. But when the day is done, with the pots dirtied, and the serving plates licked clean, Nosheteria is a part of me, and the food prepared is an extension of my kitchen.

This soup is the first recipe that I published on my blog, and now, three years later, I still make it when the first chill hits the air.

2 tablespoons unsalted butter
1 tablespoon olive oil
2 leeks, white and light green parts, sliced
2 cloves garlic, minced
1 tablespoon peeled and grated fresh ginger
salt and pepper to taste
1 teaspoon ground cinnamon
4 cups chopped butternut squash, peeled and cut into 1-inch pieces
2 green apples, cored and cut into 1-inch pieces
1 pear, cored and cut into 1-inch pieces
4 cups chicken or vegetable stock
1 tablespoon white wine (or apple cider) vinegar

In a large pot, over medium heat, melt the butter and olive oil and add the leeks. Sweat the leeks until half their volume and softened, about 5 minutes. Add the garlic and ginger and continue to sauté for 1 minute, until the ginger is fragrant. Season with salt and pepper and add the cinnamon, toasting for 2 minutes. Add the squash, apples, and pear, stirring well to ensure that they are evenly coated with the spice mixture.

Pour in the stock, bring to a boil, and taste for seasoning. Partially cover the pot and simmer for 20–25 minutes. The squash and fruit should be very tender. Remove the soup from the heat, then puree in batches until smooth. Add the vinegar and taste again for seasoning. Return the soup to the pot to heat through.

serves 4–6

Blog Appétit!

Having a blog is like having a child—a whining, fussy child who needs endless amounts of attention. At least this is how it started out for me. Suddenly I had this *thing* to watch over that had the potential to become very public. And what started the idea of becoming a blogger was that I had become a blog reader. I sat at my computer each night scanning through page after page of food blogs, each with their own take on how a meal should be prepared, until it was time to share my latest idea with Brian.

"I'm thinking of starting a blog. A food blog." I mentioned this over dinner one evening.

"Really?"

I nodded, setting my fork down. "You know how so many of the literary agents I have been querying about the cookbook say that I don't have enough of a platform? I figure this is a way to get my name out there. It's so strange—every agent wants me to be the next Rachael Ray, but I ask you: If I *were* Rachael Ray, would I still have to be querying agents in order to peddle my book?"

Brian smirked. He had heard me say this more than a few times.

"I think that's a really great idea. And it will get you writing on a regular basis, which is great." Brian, although he would never admit it, is one of those people with a can-do spirit. When we met, he was a largely self-taught jazz musician, and now he was finishing up his graduate degree in music composition. Brian is emphatic about practicing a craft—having a skill that you turn to every day, to grow with and improve upon. For him, his craft was music, and for me, it was cooking and then writing about the foods that I cooked. "So what's next? What do we have to do to get you started?"

"I called Eug, and he said he would help me out." Eugene was my sister's husband, an Englishman with a British sense of humor, technologically savvy, and most important, he had a limitless level of patience. Which no doubt would be needed in getting me started on the right track.

"All right. So what type of a food blog is it going to be?" Brian asked.

"Something simple and clean, concise—I want my blog to be similar to the kind of food that I cook. The theme will be not having a theme; I don't want to put that sort of pressure on myself. This is supposed to be fun, after all; and if it serves the purpose of boosting my platform, all the better."

If having a blog was like having a child, then entering into the blogosphere was akin to being in high school. Bloggers can be warm and welcoming, but they can also be cliquish and cruel.

I have never been a joiner. I was always the kid being shooed into the center of the classroom by my parents when all I wanted to do was sink into the sidelines. There are definitely the cool kids—bloggers with the sites that everyone reads. There are the needies—the writers who desperately want a group of readers all their own, so they comment on your site repeatedly, hoping that maybe, just maybe, you will comment back. There are the smarty-pants, with slick sites and witty writings. And then there are the normals, the mass of people with their average sites, telling of their average lives. Blogging to me was similar to how I felt in high school—constantly struggling to find my place in this microcosm of the world.

Even more specifically, there were the food blog cliques. Each of these authors had long lists of links to their brethren. There were the strictly baking blogs, writing of their latest confections. When the writer behind the Julie/Julia Project blogged her way into bookstores, so did a rash of other specific cookbook blogs. There were the vegeterian blogs, not to be confused with the vigilante vegan blogs. And there were countless gluten-free blogs espousing the wonders of teff. The international blogs (written in English) banded together like herds of ESL students eating lunch together at grubby cafeteria tables. So where did my blog, Nosheteria, fit in? I was lost in the shuffle. I didn't want to become the lone disabled food blog, my banner being the wheelchair symbol and a hamburger; I definitely wasn't ready for such a pathetic public display. So I kept my personal life to myself. The only thing left to do was to write and see what happened.

Reluctantly I joined the masses, and quickly I became obsessed. "It's so strange—it's like I'm writing into the void," I would tell

Brian when he got home from school. Frantically I would check my stats each morning, which would mark my few readers trickling in. But I had only told a select few that I was now a blogger. Placing my hand over my mouth, I would mumble those two syllables in an inaudible tone. To me, saying I was a blogger was like claiming some unpopular political party. I didn't want to be known as one of those people who couldn't get a book deal and resorted to an online medium instead. But you know what, I was. And Brian was right: writing on a regular basis was a beneficial exercise in self-reliance.

I saw a certain relief in the anonymity of blogging. For those few hundred words I composed each week, I was just Adrienne, the faceless and, more important, bodyless girl with a food blog. People weren't interested in my history—they wanted to know what I was cooking now, at that moment, and the immediacy of blogging was something that I appreciated.

There seemed to be two sides of me developing: the cook and the person. The blog was making me a better cook—more adventurous and certainly more frequent. But at the same time, I was transforming into a masterful storyteller, a grand actor, one who hid behind the words that I wrote, never revealing too much. I now had a band of loyal readers who flipped on their computers each day to find out what I had been cooking, not what my physical therapist had to say about how I was walking or what doctor had some new theory about AVMs. This selective choosing of what my readers knew was pleasing to me, even though I knew that I wasn't being entirely honest. But I was enjoying myself too much to think about it—there was food to cook!

Along with the writing came the photography—something I

had never thought much about before. I had always thought of food both as nourishment and as a beautiful object to be enjoyed before savoring. But now I had a reason to take photographic evidence of my work—my readers were eagerly waiting! Dozens of cookies would come sliding out of my oven, and as I carefully removed each treat from the baking sheet with my trusty metal spatula, I would make mental notes. "That cookie is too squat. That one is too lopsided." One would crumble and I would curse my fate. *A perfect specimen, lost,* I would think. And then the ideal cookie would arrive, after a slew of almosts and just-about-theres.

The model for my next photo shoot was tough enough to handle being roughed up yet tender enough to be tempting. And when the meal I had created was not up to par for a photo shoot, it made no difference—Brian thankfully ate it anyway. There were times, however, when my entire day had been spent in the kitchen. Recipes needed testing for the cookbook or snacks would be prepared for the latest cocktail party I was catering, and the last thing I felt like doing was cooking a dinner meal for us. But Berkeley is a marvelous place to go out and dine on the cheap—ideal for a young couple making their way in the culinary jungle.

RISING FROM BED on a weekend morning, I would plod around the apartment, waiting for the kettle of water to boil on the stove. Checking my e-mail, doing a bit of surfing on the Web, I would impatiently wait for Brian to get up. After what seemed like hours, the bedroom door would open with a sweep and my husband would come tumbling out. Usually, Brian had a gig the night before. When we first began dating, it was exciting having a boyfriend who was a musician. Frequently, Maia and I would go to see Brian play at different clubs; it gave us an excuse to go into San Francisco. We would chat with the band, never as groupies—jazz musicians didn't really have those—but as friends, and we would listen to the music. But now, these few years later, I was over it. Brian would go off to "earn some dirty be-bop money," as he liked to say, leaving me happily at home. Sometimes Lucy would stop by and we would cook dinner together, or I would go and spend time with my sister. If I was feeling particularly industrious, I would work on the cookbook or write the latest Nosheteria post. Brian would come home at the end of the night, and loosening his tie, he would tell me about his evening—the bass player who didn't show up, the trumpeter who was so drunk he played a different tune than the rest of the band. Brian was tired of being background music.

In the morning, I would wait as calmly as I could. But when that bedroom door opened, he was free game, and my bombardment began.

"Let's go out today. We should do something," I proclaimed.

"What do you have in mind?" Brian asked, rubbing the sleep from his eyes.

"We always go for brunch on Sunday, but I was thinking we should go for dim sum. It's been a while."

"Sounds good."

"Maybe we should call my parents to see if they want to come, too?"

Dim sum on Sunday mornings, lining up in a makeshift lobby, the huddled hungry masses of people, their stomachs growling in sync with the metal trolleys carrying steaming trays of Chinese delectables. I always judge a dim sum restaurant by how crowded it is, and Peony Garden was teeming. Generations of Chinese families sat around circular tables, whose centerpieces were the lazy Susans, making sharing more like a game of spinning tops than a chore, and there in the midst of all this commotion sat Brian, me, and my parents. My father rarely went out for dinner anymore; the clamor of other diners enjoying their entrées had grown to be too much for him, so a Sunday morning brunch was the perfect meal to enjoy out.

"The goal for my meal today is to eat multiple offerings of steamed pork buns and preferably a few shumai," I proclaimed, all the while keeping an eye on the carts passing around our table. Barbecued steamed pork buns had been my favorite since I was a young girl. A mediocre Chinese restaurant near my grandma's house regularly offered these savory sweet buns on their appetizer menu. Stamped with edible crimson dye, the smooth rice flour bun housed a mixture of a sweetened sauce tinged with hoisin sauce, surrounding chewy pork pieces. But the pork buns at Peony Garden were unlike any I had tasted before. The pork was sumptuous; the fat had been stewed away, leaving behind rich pork flavor; and the rice flour buns were light and cloud-like.

"I think that can be arranged; we'll all be on the lookout," said my mom.

As I had improved mentally and physically over the years since my AVM, my father had declined. My mom pulled out the chair for him and guided him to take his seat. He sat between my mom and me, staring intently as the carts began passing. Crisply fried orbs of gluten rolled in sesame seeds encased a sticky black bean paste; oodles of noodles slithered by, accented with garlic chives; fried balls of chopped crab and shrimp meat were stabbed messily with crab claws. We grabbed our favorites from the carts and inquired about unique arrivals. Now a left-handed chopstick user, I plucked dumplings from a platter with my sticks and set them on my dad's plate, watching him struggle to use his chopsticks.

"So, Brian, how does it feel to be almost finished with school?" my mom asked between bites of shrimp and pork shumai.

"Don't even ask. I feel like I have been in school forever, and for what?" Brian's tenure at Berkeley was coming to a close, and he had been furiously applying for jobs at universities around the country but had heard nothing. We were beginning to feel like the ignored couple, he from academic institutions and me from literary agents. But still we plugged away.

"Something is bound to happen for you. I have a good feeling about you both."

"Well, thanks. I'm glad you have such confidence in my abilities," Brian replied.

"There they are," I proclaimed. "My buns!" I caught a glimpse of the steam cart emerging from the kitchen and flailed my arm wildly to signal the server.

"Easy there, it's coming this way," remarked Brian.

"I know; I've just been waiting. I want to make sure I still have some room left to eat them." And I did, but after the countless mouthfuls of other dim sum specialties, my goal of eating more than a few pork buns would have to wait until my next trip to Peony Garden. I savored the taste of one perfect bun.

• • •

"TASTE THIS," I commanded Brian, following him around with a spoonful of pork filling. Since that Sunday, I had been trying to recreate the steamed pork bun filling from Peony Garden.

"Mmm, it's good."

"How good? Good like you *want* to eat more or good like you *have* to eat more?"

"What? I don't know. What is this for, blog or book?"

This was a very common question, as my world had become consumed with recipes both for the blog and for my burgeoning cookbook. Luckily, Brian was understanding.

Writing a cookbook was a bit like giving birth, or like what I *imagine* giving birth to be like. There were times when a devised recipe wouldn't please me. Again and again, I would try it, until I grew absolutely sick of the ingredients. Writing a recipe became a labor—a tremendous amount of work over a long gestation period. But in the end, there was the joy that comes with creating something out of nothing and something that could live on without my physical assistance. If I created a delicious recipe, with insights about the food that was being prepared and hints about preparation, it was possible that this recipe would become a favorite to someone else. I wanted that possibility.

I had been an avid cookbook collector for quite some time. Plunk me down in a good used bookstore, with its musty shelves groaning under the weight of countless volumes of cookbook titles, and I will browse for hours, finding a much-loved copy of *Beard on Bread*, or a recipe for soupy dal, flavored with cumin and accented with chopped tomato, in a forgotten hippie cookbook from the sixties. Eventually, I'd buy a few cookbooks and bring them home. The mark of an avid cookbook collector is

179

staying up too late, dog-earing the pages of enticing recipes with beautiful photographs and fragrant-sounding spices. Then there is a careful selection of which new recipes to try and a rush to the market the following day. You fill your cart with bulbs of fennel, rosy radishes, and fillets of pure white fish to embellish with knobs of creamy unsalted butter. You are ready to make this recipe!

You toil—chop and slice, season and roast. And then, sometimes the recipe doesn't turn out. Your fish is not flaky, and where is that glistening bit of butter? Your fillet looks nothing like the picture on page 80. Actually, your fish is pathetic and insipid. You are disappointed, saddened; you place that book back on the shelf only to glance through it a few times more, just to look at the pretty pictures. Maybe you even sell it back to the used bookstore from which you bought it.

I knew this feeling well—the anticipation and the excitement, only to be let down. I did not want this to happen to my book. Sitting at my computer, right hand resting calmly in my lap and left hand furiously typing the introductions to each recipe, the little tidbits of information giving the home cook helpful hints and reassurances came flowing out. The recipes had to be perfect. I did not want readers to find themselves in hair-raising culinary disappointments. So I cooked and tasted. Brian, Lucy, Frank, and others became my guinea pigs. I wanted my diners to honestly assess the food they ate at my house. My kitchen became a laboratory of cooking.

Was that a half teaspoon or a full teaspoon? Would this recipe be more flavorful with chicken stock rather than water? These questions were of grave importance to me now. They had to be answered correctly, and this gave me a new sense of purpose. I was becoming a writer and a cook. I proceeded to write the cookbook with one thing in mind: life can be disappointing enough, so let the food that you eat be simple, trustworthy, and delicious.

CHAPTER 15

Tandoori Chicken Sandwich

The Tandoori Chicken Sandwich—perfection in a fusion meal. Who would have thought that you could find this delicious assemblage of Indian ingredients wrapped in naan bread along the side of I-80, in El Sobrante, California, at a place called Tandoori Chicken USA? I loved this restaurant, if you can even call it that.

It has since, very sadly, closed down, having a solid fourteen-year run, leaving me Tandoori Chicken Sandwich-less. So I have devised this recipe that recalls each ingredient used to make that sandwich, even the spicy yogurt-mint sauce. It is not the Tandoori Chicken Sandwich from Tandoori Chicken USA, but it runs a pretty close second.

FOR THE TANDOORI
CHICKEN:
4 boneless, skinless chicken
   breast halves
I lemon
½ teaspoon salt
I teaspoon ground cumin
½ teaspoon ground
   coriander
½ teaspoon paprika
½ teaspoon turmeric
¼ teaspoon cayenne pepper
¼ teaspoon garam masala*
I cup plain yogurt
I tablespoon grated fresh
   ginger
I large clove garlic, minced

*Garam masala is an Indian spice blend including warm spices, such as cardamom, cinnamon, and cloves. If you have difficulty finding this blend, substitute any one of these spices.

Score the flesh of the chicken diagonally, making ½-inch incisions, 1 inch apart. In a shallow, nonreactive baking pan, squeeze the lemon on the chicken breast halves, season with salt, and set aside.

In a small, dry frying pan, over medium heat, toast the cumin, coriander, paprika, turmeric, cayenne pepper, and garam masala until fragrant, about 2 minutes. Transfer to a large bowl and stir in the yogurt, ginger, and garlic. Pour the yogurt mixture over the chicken breasts, covering well with the marinade. Cover the pan and place in the refrigerator for a minimum of 8 hours, or overnight.

Preheat the oven to 350°F. Remove the chicken from the marinade, brushing the excess yogurt mixture from the surface of the chicken. In a grill pan, over high heat, sear the chicken on both sides; the chicken should have dark grill marks. Transfer the chicken to a baking dish and bake for 15–20 minutes, or until the juices run clear. Or, if you wish, you can barbecue the chicken.

Set the chicken aside to rest while the other components of the sandwich are made.

FOR THE MINT SAUCE:
½ serrano or other spicy green chili
¼ cup fresh mint leaves
½ teaspoon salt
1 cup plain yogurt

Cut the top of the chili off and discard. In a blender combine all of the sauce ingredients and pulse until smooth. The sauce should be pale green and slightly watery from blending.

FOR THE SANDWICHES:
1 recipe tandoori chicken
4 frozen naan breads, reheated as instructed on package

2 cups coarsely chopped romaine lettuce
1 recipe mint sauce

Cut the chicken into quarter-inch slices and set aside. Take one piece of naan bread and place approximately one-quarter of the lettuce on half of the piece of bread. Douse liberally with the mint sauce. Add the chicken slices from one breast half and top with additional mint sauce. Fold the naan bread over as if you were making a taco. Complete the process with the additional pieces of naan, making four sandwiches total.

makes 4 sandwiches

Road Food

Bryce was getting married. It was a typical spring day in Berkeley—foggy and brisk in the morning hours, burning off to a clear day, with the rays of sun softly warming your back in the afternoon. His bride was nervous. Her grown daughters, standing together as bridesmaids, looked like a pastel parade, and Bryce was excited. So excited I could not get him out of the church's dank kitchen. Or maybe Bryce was nervous as well. I have found that many people like to hide out in the kitchen during anxious times. I know that I did when anxiety got the best of me. But having a groom looming over me, pulling on his cuff links and peering over my shoulder as I placed French breakfast radishes with a sprinkling of coarse sea salt on the crudité platters, was hardly a settling activity for me, either.

I had amassed a small client base for dinner parties and small events, but as a rule I didn't cater weddings. Bryce was the exception. How could I say no to the man who gave me my start in catering? And this wedding was different, but perhaps that was the problem. I wasn't the caterer per se—I was the navigator. The wedding was a family affair; Bryce and his bride-to-be had delegated much of the food preparation to their extended family, who were only too happy to help. They had handed out recipes in the weeks prior to the wedding for the food of their choice. I was hired to make a few choice hors d'oeuvres, but mostly to receive piles of food made by cousins, arrange them on platters, and then set these platters out on the gargantuan buffet table in the reception hall. It sounded like a small task when I initially talked with Bryce, but as I stood in the kitchen, on the receiving end of the food line, I was all too happy that I had recruited my mother and my sister to help me with this event.

"Where do you want these?" asked an eager aunt.

"What do you have?" I asked, still calm because the deluge had yet to begin.

"These!" she said, tearing off the foil that covered a slumping batch of stuffed mushrooms.

"Okay, thanks. I'll take those," I said, putting the tired mushrooms down on the counter next to a crudité platter that I prepared, which looked straight from the field in comparison.

Over the next hour came plate after plate of family specialties. There were savory cheesecakes accented with pepper jelly, corn fritters glistening from the oil they were fried in, crumbled homemade blue cheese crisps, and candied nuts practically bursting from their sugary shells. The never-forgotten rows of stuffed mushroom caps jockeyed for space. It was clear that these were family favorites, but I wondered: Who had thought to put these foods together? There was no cohesion, no thought put into this assemblage.

"Look at all of these cheesecakes. Are they even from the same recipe?" my sister asked.

I glanced down at the half-dozen cheesecakes lined up on the counter. It was true; each looked like a completely unique meal. When preparing the cheesecakes, some people had used chunky preserves, others a smooth jelly. One cheesecake with the jelly smeared on top appeared to have the condiment only as an afterthought. There were short cakes, cakes baked in pie plates, and one, hardly holding its shape, seemed not to have been baked at all. "Yep, they're all from the same recipe," I said, shaking my head. "It's amazing how one recipe can be interpreted in so many different ways."

There was a lot of one-armed pointing that day. My poor mother looked as though she had run a marathon as I watched her blot the sweat that had collected above her lip repeatedly throughout the day, and my sister—who doesn't even like to cook—was a trouper as she brought empty plates of savory cheesecake back into the kitchen. "Well, I guess the guests didn't really care that each cake was entirely different from the next. They ate everything," she said.

"I guess if I have learned anything from catering, it is that everyone's palate is completely different. One person's chili cheese fry is another person's foie gras with toast points," I said, placing the final load of dishes into the industrial dishwasher. "Never again, though. I think that I made a good decision by keeping my catering company small—it's hard work."

"Well, I guess hard work does pay off," I said incredulously.

"I know. I still can't believe it," Brian said, shaking his head slowly back and forth like a dog with a chew toy.

Brian and I were driving up I-80, making the first of many trips to our storage unit—a storage unit that would house much of our worldly possessions for at least the next two years. We were moving to New York City. Brian got a postdoctoral fellowship in the Music Department at Columbia University, and not a minute too soon. Things had been looking bleak. The academic year was racing to a close and there were few prospects on the horizon. Each day, Brian would race home a mass of nerves and sit in front of the computer to check for job listings. It was getting harder for him to believe what everyone had been telling him—*something* would come through. But just as I had found an agent—in New York, no less—Brian's luck was turning around, too. A sudden interview in New York, and two days later, a phone call with a job offer. The announcement of the postdoc meant that both our lives were about to change dramatically. However, it was possible that our move to New York would be a temporary one. But after Bryce's wedding, my frustration of not having control over what foods were made, and watching my mom and my sister sweat from exhaustion, made me wonder whether catering was beginning to run its course, too. I was ready for all the changes that New York would bring.

Running straight and wide, I-80 had become my yellow brick road of sorts, carrying me to and from the various destinations in my life. It connected small cities on the peninsula, like Hillsborough, with Vallejo, and Berkeley lay in between.

"Are you hungry?" asked Brian.

"I could eat something. Maybe we should go to Tandoori Chicken USA."

"Perfect. I could definitely eat one of their sandwiches to celebrate our move."

The car rocked and bumped as we exited the freeway in the unincorporated town of El Sobrante, a forgotten part of the East Bay with many storage units, mobile home parks, and hole-in-the-wall restaurants located in strip malls. Coming from California, nonchain restaurants in strip malls hold a special place in my heart. Usually they signify a little piece of a quickly diminishing American dream—a chance to own your own business. We stopped at a traffic light, and in the distance I could see it, across the street from a Thrift Town clothing store near a nameless Mexican restaurant. It looked as though this family-owned Indian restaurant had been thrown together in a hurry, but it made no difference to me. The care was found in the food rather than the decor. Once an old drive-in Dairy Queen restaurant, with glass hanging lights illuminating the rickety booths and stained linoleum floors, now flyers of advertisements for Taj Majal beer and loose kernels of basmati rice were left behind at each table to blow in the wind like aromatic tumbleweeds.

"What are you going to have?" Brian asked me, as if he didn't know the answer to such a mundane question.

I smiled in recognition to the woman behind the counter taking our order. She spoke with a soft and lilting Indian accent. The menu tacked to the wall on the front counter was superfluous as I ordered my usual—a tandoori chicken sandwich and, ignoring the advertisements for various beers, a small cherry Coke. This restaurant was one of the few with syrupy sweet cherry Coke flowing out of the fountain. In moments, the sandwiches arrived, a kaleidoscope of brightly spiced color. Tender pieces of tandoori chicken breast, piquantly noted with smoky cumin, bright cayenne pepper, golden turmeric, and flavorful ginger, rested warmly on a bed of crisp romaine lettuce leaves. The mixture was then doused in a complex mint sauce that married the flavors together perfectly. Wrapped in homemade naan bread, prepared expertly in a traditional clay oven, there it was—perfection in a sandwich. I hungrily took a bite and said, "I will *definitely* miss this place."

Getting into the car, satiated by my midday meal, I took the final sips of my soda, feeling the gentle burn of carbonation as the liquid went down. I nodded to the cartoon eggplant painted on the front window of the restaurant, beckoning patrons to come inside to eat a sandwich, and maybe have a warming dish of *bhartha* as well. I knew that I would be back, I just wasn't sure when.

"Maybe we should take a tour of the 80, as a kind of last hurrah to the Bay Area before we leave," I said, flipping on the car radio and settling in for the ride back to our apartment.

"You know we're here for another two months, don't you?" Brian asked.

"Yes, but who knows when we will both have an entire day with nothing to do? Soon there will be an entire apartment to pack up and many more trips to our storage unit with boxes full of our lives."

"That's very maudlin of you," Brain said with a chuckle. "Okay, where to?"

"Ranch 99, of course."

Located in the Pacific East Mall, an amalgamation of all things

Asian, stands Ranch 99, an enormous Chinese supermarket with stores throughout California. I would frequent this market monthly when I was in need of anything Asian or in search of Asian inspiration to my usual California-fresh ingredients. Inside, the fluorescent lights made the produce look almost clinical, but upon closer look, you realized you were in vegetable heaven. There were countless Chinese greens: bok choy, choy sum, and water spinach lay next to winter melons and gourds of all sorts.

"I suppose I shouldn't buy too much here. I'll be trying to empty the refrigerator soon. Maybe coming to Ranch 99 wasn't the best idea," I said.

Ranch 99 had become a well-kept catering secret of mine. In Berkeley, there are such stupendous markets, stores where the produce is impeccably gathered in each season, waiting to be brought home. Sometimes I thought the residents forgot about these relatively new markets. However, this oversight worked out well for me, as I was able to find amazing foodstuffs on the cheap. In the wintertime, I made edible centerpieces for dining tables out of handfuls of kumquats and clementines, waking up diners with their citrus fragrance. I found row after row of mismatched Asian teacups that had beauty in their discord, and favorite utensils like my bamboo spider to dip into hot oil and retrieve the latest glistening fritter.

We trudged on to the condiment aisle, where jar upon jar stood with vials and bottles like a Dickensian apothecary shop. This aisle of the Ranch was a particular favorite of Frank's; he was the condiment king. If one condiment was good, five were better. I had some of these jars at home, chilling in the fridge. I purchased them on a whim, thinking that I would cook so often with that jar of fermented black beans, but now they ruminated, continuing to grow more fermented with each passing week.

Lucy and Frank had particularly loved the Pacific East Mall. "It's unlike any other American mall I know, and I've known many growing up in the San Fernando Valley, the birthplace of the shopping mall," Lucy would say. "It's so well lit, with shiny floors. And where else can you get both Chinese herbs and Vietnamese hot pots?"

Brian and I left Ranch 99 to wander around the mall, but this time on our own. I was unencumbered from packages, and we did not have our animated shopping companions, Lucy and Frank. I was still slow, but not the slowest shopper.

"Let's get those egg puffs—I love them." Brian and I arrived at the vendor who sold milky bubble teas with gelatinous orbs of chewy tapioca. In the back of the tea-making operation was a peculiar multisphere waffle iron. I ordered one portion of egg puffs and watched as an embarrassed young man wearing a quilted apron and matching cap poured the batter into the iron with a sizzle. Upon contact with the heat, the batter lost its sheen and began to bubble before the lid to the iron was dropped on top. Steam erupted, and in a moment's time, the puffs were complete. They came pouring out of the iron and into a crisp paper bag. The bag softened with the moisture of the puffs, and I quickly reached inside and pulled out a small puff, no bigger than a golf ball. Barely kissed with sugar, the batter was an eggy concoction and tasted like custard, only with a thin, chewy skin. "Mmm, why are these puffs so good? There's practically nothing to them," I said to Brian.

"I'm not really sure. Maybe it's because you know that you could never make them at home."

I grabbed another puff while Brian held on to the bag. "Well, good-bye Pacific East Mall, good-bye Ranch 99, and good-bye egg puff man. I'm off."

"Okay, now *that* is maudlin," said Brian with a laugh.

"It's for dramatic effect. We're on to bigger things—I hope."

CHAPTER 16

Springtime Frittata with Peas and Mint

I have not always been an egg lover; I have not always even been an egg eater, but it was the frittata that first made me a fan. When baked in a frittata, the egg becomes a vehicle for whatever other savory items the dish contains. It is perfect for egg skeptics, as well as devotees. This frittata is bright and springy, although utilizing frozen peas makes it a year-round treasure. A bit untraditional, it is not flipped but is finished off in the broiler, with dollops of fromage blanc. This is a spoonable, creamy cheese, with a delicate, milky tang, but ricotta cheese can also be used if you have difficulty finding fromage blanc. Frittatas are one of the first foods that Maia and I bonded over, so cooking them will always hold special memories for me.

10 eggs
salt and pepper to taste
1 tablespoon unsalted butter
2 tablespoons olive oil
1 cup thinly sliced leeks, white and light green parts only

1 cup peas (thawed if using frozen, blanched if using fresh)
3 tablespoons coarsely chopped fresh mint
½ cup fromage blanc or ricotta cheese

Preheat the broiler. In a medium-size bowl, whisk the eggs until well blended, and season well with salt and pepper. Set aside.

In a 10-inch skillet that is safe for the broiler, over medium

197

heat, melt the butter and olive oil. Add the leeks, season lightly with salt and pepper, and sweat until soft and translucent, about 5 minutes. Add the peas and 2 tablespoons of mint and sauté briefly. Pour in the eggs. With a heatproof rubber spatula, cook the eggs, gently scrambling, to obtain loose, small curds. Move the cooked eggs to the center of the pan, allowing the uncooked portion to set along the sides. Do this several times, until most of the eggs are half set, 5–7 minutes.

Turn the heat off. Spoon small, quarter-size dollops of fromage blanc randomly on the surface of the egg mixture. Place the skillet under the broiler until the frittata gets puffy and toasty brown, and the fromage blanc begins to color, 6–7 minutes. Remove from the broiler, sprinkle with the remaining tablespoon of chopped mint, and enjoy either warm or at room temperature.

serves 6

The Big Apples

I came to New York in July with only two goals in mind: to find an apartment and to meet my agent. The city could swirl around me; the subways could whiz by; the skyscrapers could loom ever larger, casting their shadows on the thousands of people scurrying like ants at a picnic in Bryant Park; the vendors standing over sweltering steamers of hot dogs at their carts could sell their snacks to someone else—I had a mission.

Brian and I had been warned about Manhattan real estate before we came. I had heard the stories of someone's roommate's sister's brother-in-law who came to New York with the intention of striking it big on Broadway and was now sharing a studio apartment with three castmates from the off-off-off-off-Broadway show he was an understudy for, and the five-pound sewer rat that the exterminator had been unable to get rid of that this person now had as a pet. Oh, and he was paying $2,000 a month for the privilege.

I swore that this would not happen to Brian and me. The weeks before we left for our informative premove visit to Manhattan, I stayed up late into the night researching apartments on Craigslist. "Here's one," I would call out to Brian, who had gotten home from a gig in San Francisco: "Charming one bedroom, overlooking the park, close to transportation . . . and it's in our price range. It's a little far from school for you, 145th and Amsterdam, and Columbia's on what, 116th and Broadway? But still . . . I'm going to call Maia tomorrow."

Maia had moved to New York City with Gabe soon after graduating from Berkeley. They had lived in their fair share of New York City oddities—picture a bathroom where you have to step up to reach the toilet—before moving out of the city and into Brooklyn for a little bit of quiet and a whole lot of space. Besides being a dear friend, that summer, premove, Maia became my go-to, New York real estate girl. She and Gabe had become experts at translating real estate jargon. "I don't know if you want that apartment, Adrienne. Charming is usually real estate code for tiny, and what park is that ad referring to? Central Park ends at 110th; they must be talking about some little neighborhood play-ground. I don't know about that. And 145th? That's kind of far. I've only been up to those parts like three times, and I've lived in New York for five years now. Besides, it's still early to be looking; I'm sure you'll find something. I'll help you when you get here." Click.

THE WHEELS OF the plane jumped and skidded to a grinding stop on the tarmac of JFK airport. "Good evening, folks. It's 10:17 eastern standard time, in New York City, and eighty-two degrees.

Welcome home, or have a nice trip. Thanks for flying with us."

"Eighty-two degrees at ten o'clock at night? We never would get that at home," I remarked incredulously.

"Well, this is our home now. Or it will be very soon," Brian said as he placed his hand over my right hand and gave it a squeeze. He knew that I couldn't respond with a clenching squeeze in return, but when he looked over at me, peering out the window of the 747, he could feel my excitement.

Maia and Gabe picked us up at the airport. We hadn't seen them since our wedding six months ago. I looked down at my left hand and the broad gold band that had been scratched and dulled in the short time that I wore it. Once gleaming, it now had a pleasant shine. There were scratches evident from fumbling around in the kitchen; fissure-like marks had erupted on the bottom surface, telling stories of me gripping the handle of my chef's knife and setting to work.

Maia came barreling out of the car to greet Brian and me with enormous hugs. "Oh my god! I can't believe it! You're here! It is completely possible that we could be neighbors," she exclaimed.

"Well, we're not here yet. But we will be in about a month. That hardly seems possible," I said, turning to Brian and shaking my head.

"Well, let's go back to our place, get you guys settled, and you can have something to eat," Maia offered, tucking her arm through mine as she had done so many times before. It had been far too long since I had seen her. She was engaged now, and she was growing her hair out for her wedding. But wearing her black rubber flip-flops and a casual summer dress, she was the same girl who had been through so much with me. We scrunched in the backseat of their little Toyota, and Gabe, who had been driving in New York for years, fearlessly zipped onto the Brooklyn–Queens Expressway.

Maia showed me her ring and prattled on about being done with the bar exam. I remember nodding a lot and offering the occasional "Really?" but there is little else about our car conversation that I remember. I was too busy taking it all in. The scenery from the freeway is not always indicative of how a place truly is, and airport drives are usually not the most picturesque. But as Gabe deftly changed lanes, rocking all of the passengers from side to side in the car, I grew increasingly wary.

Off in the distance, I could see the bright lights of Manhattan. The Chrysler Building stood like a beacon of the Art Deco era that once was, its spire struggling to stand tall among the nameless buildings of the skyline. But as we zoomed past countless row houses, with their shabby awnings groaning under the weight of the starless night sky, and air conditioners sighing out cool air and dripping sludge that collected in dank pools under the windows, I rested my head on the back of the seat.

Finally we exited the freeway. "So this is Williamsburg," Maia said. "I never thought we would live here, but we found a really great place. It feels so enormous after all of the tiny, junior one-bedrooms we lived in all over Manhattan. And, Adrienne, the kitchen is huge; it's big enough to fit a large dining table. I am proud to say, I am now the owner/renter of my first full-size stove since we moved to New York."

I felt like we were off-roading in some all-terrain vehicle as Gabe turned down bumpy roads filled with potholes and loose gravel. I had heard about Williamsburg—it was gritty and trendy, with hipsters and an underground music scene, none of which particularly interested me. But I never imagined it to be this bad. It was brimming with disaffected youths spilling out of neighborhood bars. Boys in their tight tapered jeans, tucked into Converse high-tops, wore ironic T-shirts with "*Not* In a Band" and "My Mother Went to Brooklyn and All She Got Me Was This Stupid Condo" emblazoned on the front. Their thumbs poked jauntily through holes at the hemline of their T-shirts as they stood drinking beer, only *looking* like they didn't care about what everyone else was doing. Girls stood around, sporting the latest modern mullet hairdo. Their eighties-style rompers were nipped in at the waist with an elasticized belt acting as control-top panty hose for their swelling beer bellies. These kids were too cool for school. I glanced at Brian in the darkened backseat. He too was gazing out the window, taking it all in. I couldn't see his face, and I wondered if he felt the same way I did. Driving down Bedford Avenue, even I felt old at the ripe age of twenty-seven. The social pressure was too much for me to bear. Before even seeing Maia and Gabe's apartment, Williamsburg was definitely a no. But thinking about finding a place would have to wait; I was tired and hungry, and felt the need to stand with my feet on New York ground.

In college, Maia had been my cooking buddy. We learned together. Like so many of our peers who had been fed and nurtured by their families at home, there were gaps in our culinary knowledge waiting to be filled. But just as school introduced us to the writings of Chaucer, Milton, Dostoyevsky, and Nabokov, being in college and living away from home forced us to create our first kitchens. I had eaten many chicken breasts, basted, marinated, or seasoned by my mother, but as I slipped my own chicken breast into the oven for the first time, I had to keep glancing at the recipe that I had torn out of a magazine the week before. I read the instructions over, time and again. I flicked the oven light on and off so many times, I feared that I would burn out the lightbulb. And still, I needed to telephone my mother to ask her the cardinal question: "But how do I know when it's done?" Cooking, like many other skills, is something to be learned and honed over time.

When I think of Maia, I think of frittatas: versatile, functional, delicious. It was our junior year at Berkeley; we had unwittingly signed up for a wretched, touchy-feely, "talk about what this book really means" seminar. Maia, ever diligent, had showed up for each class, notebook in hand, and attempted to take notes about what people were saying (really *saying*) in Chapter XYZ. I had written the class off weeks into it. I attended but only on a perfunctory level. The professor was a tiny woman with cropped hair who carried a worn JanSport backpack stuffed with crumpled paperback novels. Some students loved her, hanging on her every soft-spoken, politically correct word. I mostly wondered how she managed to wear the same too-large, drop-waist dress every class. My attendance in that class faltered, and when I did attend, I sat in the creaky desk/chair combination and gazed out the window at my fellow students bustling by as the minutes slowly ticked on the standard-issue school clock.

Come finals month, the professor—continuing with the feel-good nature of the seminar—decided to have a roundtable graded discussion on all of the books we had read to date. "I was thinking, in the spirit of sharing in a lively discussion, we would also want to share food. I can't think of a more intimate way to share than to break bread together. So, on finals day, come to class ready to share your thoughts and ready to share your food," our professor practically whispered.

"I can think of a few things more intimate than breaking bread together," I said to Maia as soon as we were out of the classroom. "But whatever. So what do you want to make?" I asked.

"I don't know, maybe a frittata. Something we can cut up and that is easily transportable."

"Sounds perfect . . . but is it intimate enough?"

On finals day, a collection of desks were pushed together, forming an odd buffet table, with a perimeter of chairs, restricting diners. Even odder than the makeshift table was the assortment of food that had been assembled, waiting to be consumed. From the less than culinarily inclined, there were generic bags of corn chips and jars of salsa with vaguely Mexican-sounding names. Bags of mini-carrots sat, still moist with condensation from the refrigerator. There was a curious Israeli couscous salad, overflowing with chopped peppers, slivers of green onion, and drowning in a quagmire of bottled Italian dressing. Due to more than a few people bringing in trays of messily frosted cupcakes, doused with brightly colored sprinkles, the buffet table was remarkably imbalanced; and off in the corner, next to the Wailing Wall of desk chairs, sat the one edible, in my opinion, item—our frittata.

Rather untraditionally, Maia and I had baked the frittata entirely in a large Pyrex pan. This ensured that neat geometrical squares could be cut, rather than wobbly semicircular pieces, as they would have been if the frittata had been made in the usual skillet. There is something so simple yet impressive about a frittata. Even a bad one, made with little care, no cheese, and vegetables scraped from the bottom of the tender, is good. "What's that?" questioned a classmate.

"It's a frittata," Maia answered, her words met with a blank stare. "It's like a giant baked omelet."

"Oh. I'm a vegan," said the girl, reeking of essential oils.

Despite our efforts, we went home that afternoon with a half-eaten tray of frittata.

It was after eleven o'clock when we arrived at Maia and Gabe's Williamsburg apartment. "Your room is at the end of the hallway, next to the bathroom. I whipped up a little something before we left for the airport, in case you guys were hungry. I'll meet you in the kitchen."

Plopping down our stuff in the spare bedroom, I looked at Brian. He seemed weary from the flight. "Let's go see what Maia has made. We should probably eat a little something." We walked into the kitchen. Gabe was sitting at the table, drinking a beer. Maia was right; it was an enormous table, seating at least eight. Maia was standing at the stove over a heavy cast-iron skillet that appeared to weigh more than she did.

"I made a frittata. And there's bruschetta on the table," she said, slipping the knife unencumbered through the puffed, baked egg mixture and cutting us all slices.

"Perfect." And it *was* perfect, a familiar food in an altogether unfamiliar place. There is something to be said for history, and Maia and I had quite a history together. Our lives had definitely diverged. The bulk of our adult lives had now been lived away from each other, and we had grown into a tax attorney and a fledgling food writer. That night, we sat around the table together, pushing bits of egg around the blue ceramic plates that looked familiar to me—like ones that Maia had owned in Berkeley. It was late and the conversation dwindled as the nighttime hours advanced. But despite sitting at an unfamiliar table in an unfamiliar city, I felt at home at Maia's house. She was the girl I was with when I first met Brian, the girl whose arm I so often took while walking side by side, and the girl with whom I had made my very first frittata.

Sitting there with my husband and Maia, an old friend in a new city, I thought—*This is it, the beginning of the next phase of my life.*

CHAPTER 17

Haute Egg Sandwich

The handheld egg breakfast sandwich is ubiquitous in New York. When I moved to Manhattan, I had my share. Made at the griddle of the local bodega, they range from a delicious and cheap breakfast morsel to a barely edible means of getting a bit of morning nourishment. Here is my homage to the egg sandwich with a decidedly elegant bent. With Gorgonzola cheese and fresh pear, it leans toward haute cuisine, but it is still an infinitely portable play on the same old egg sandwich.

4 eggs
3 tablespoons milk
salt and pepper to taste
1 tablespoon unsalted butter
½ tablespoon olive oil
⅓ cup crumbled Gorgonzola
  or blue cheese

4 English muffins, split and
  toasted
2 tablespoons honey
1 pear, very thinly sliced

Whisk the eggs and milk together and season with salt and pepper. In a medium-size skillet, over low heat, melt the butter and olive oil together. Add the egg mixture, and stirring constantly, scramble until the eggs have just set and small curds have developed, 2–3 minutes. Turn off the heat and sprinkle the cheese evenly over the eggs. Do not mix in.

Arrange the toasted English muffins. Spread honey on the

bottom half of each muffin, about ½ tablespoon per sandwich. Add the sliced pear, evenly dividing between each sandwich. Sprinkle with a healthy dose of pepper. Spoon egg onto each sandwich; the cheese should be slightly melted by now. Top with the other half of the muffin, and dash out the door.

makes 4 sandwiches

Fast Food

So, you know where you're going, right?" asked Maia for the umpteenth time that morning.

"I have the address, I know where the subway station is, and I've given myself plenty of time," I said.

"And you can always ask. New Yorkers are really helpful."

"Okay, wish me luck," I said, scooting out the front door. Brian was spending the morning apartment hunting, and I was going to meet my agent. It all sounded so official. It was July in New York and you could feel the impending heat, ready to strike in full force during the middle of the day. I strolled down Bedford Avenue to the station, stopping at a twenty-four-hour deli to pick up a bottle of water. Herds of hipsters were assembled in clumps near the deli counter, ordering their morning meals: "Egg-and-cheese-on-a-roll, coffee—black." "Large coffee—light." "Bacon-egg-and-cheese-on-a-roll, coffee—milk, two sugars." The short-order cooks were working furiously behind the counter. They worked as fast as the orders came in, flinging foil-wrapped sandwiches across the counter to be rung up. My stomach felt like coils from a chain-link fence, wrapped tightly from nerves. I didn't think that it could handle ingesting much more than cool water, so I placed my bottle silently on the counter, paid, and left the deli anonymously.

Waiting for the Manhattan-bound L train, I could feel the perspiration begin to collect at the nape of my neck and was all too happy when the train came whooshing by, creating a warm breeze in the station. The train stopped and the doors rushed open. Cold air spilled out of the train along with countless passengers, heads nodding to the beat of their iPods, newspapers tucked messily under their arms.

Inside, the car felt like a morgue, with people chilling coolly on the subway seats. Stepping onto the train, I found a seat, noticing the many different riders of the subway. There were the ubiquitous iPod listeners; readers, noses buried in the text, eyes darting along the page; stockbrokers scanning through pages of e-mail on their BlackBerries; and women putting on entire faces of makeup, never once poking themselves in the eye with a mascara wand when the train came to a screeching halt. There was a homeless man sitting by himself in a seat for two, eating a meal of tuna fish from a foil pouch. With a plastic knife, he dipped into the bag of fish, then slid the knife between his eagerly awaiting lips. Even though the entire car stunk of stale tuna fish, I could tolerate it—he so enjoyed his meal—this was his egg and cheese on a roll.

When the subway lurched to a stop, it tossed the people who had not had the luck of finding a seat from side to side. The doors slid open smoothly and they were off! Passengers veritably ran from the train to begin the upward climb toward the street. Each flight of stairs is preparation for the pace of the city. New York is not a city of meanderers. I wanted to call out, "Slow down! What is your hurry? So what if you are a split second late?" But I didn't; I probably wouldn't have been heard in the rush of all the people.

By the time I reached the Upper East Side, I was frazzled from the ride. The train had stopped midjourney for some unknown reason. The intercom clicked on and the jumbled voice of the conductor was heard but not understood by the passengers. When the tracks cleared and the train crawled on to the next station, I decided to get off one stop prior to my destination. I had forty-five minutes to walk the eleven blocks to my agent's office, which definitely seemed doable.

Climbing the stairs leading to the street, I gripped the hand-rail with my left hand. I felt like a driver on the wrong side of the road as would-be travelers barreled down the steps around me, hurrying to catch their trains. I muttered, "Excuse me," "Pardon me," and "I'm sorry," shaking my head, but no one seemed to care; so on I trudged. Above ground, I was met with bright sunlight and a blast of heat and mugginess that smelled of sweat and trash. It was the same temperature outside as it was in the underground labyrinths of the subway. I was not used to this heat. I glanced down at my ankles, turning crimson from the heat, pumping hot blood down into my toes. My feet were starting to swell, and the red flats I had worn, my most attractive walking shoes, were starting to chafe, creating voluminous blisters with each step. I blinked several times, as my eyes adjusted to the bright sunlight.

So this was the tony Upper East Side. Huge buildings towered above me, each home to countless New Yorkers, but their inhabitants were hard at work in the concrete jungle. Nannies pushed strollers with children munching from baggies of Cheerios. They stopped at street corners, waiting for the light to change, and toyed with umbrellas attached to the strollers, desperate to keep the burning sun off of the children's faces. School was out for the summer, and I passed hordes of preteen girls wearing gallons of eyeliner, sucking down frozen Starbucks drinks.

I felt too old for Williamsburg, and as I looked at all of the moneyed families, too young for the Upper East Side. Peering down Lexington Avenue, I attempted to get my bearings. The street seemed to go on forever, the awnings of various shops dwarfed by the looming apartment buildings. With the city's children swarming around me, this did not seem like a neighborhood where any agent would have a place of business, but I shrugged off the growing questions as I walked up the block.

I arrived at the neoclassical building on Park Avenue. Its brick facade had the cool look of the forties.

"I'm here to see Suzanne Short," I told the spritely elderly man working at the front desk. He looked so welcoming, wearing a rumpled polyester suit that matched the front awning of the building.

"Of course. Floor fourteen, apartment twelve."

"Thanks." I walked to the elevator, my shoes looking dull and scuffed in comparison to the gleaming marble tiles of the floor. Once inside the elevator, I exhaled loudly, placing my left hand squarely on my stomach. It rumbled curtly. I was a bundle of nerves. The elevator climbed upward as I said, "This is it," to no one but myself.

I was early by ten minutes. I let the minutes tick by for as long as I could stand it in the hallway near Suzanne's front door. I paced as best I could, letting my right foot meet my left. I was performing a sort of wedding march, but this was the agent's march. At three minutes to the hour, I could wait no longer, so I pressed the buzzer. I waited, and waited some more, then pressed again. Still no answer. "Please don't tell me that I have the wrong day," I said. I knocked and this time heard shuffling behind the door. It flew open suddenly.

"A-drienne, right? It's so nice that you could stop by. The buzzer doesn't work . . . hasn't for years. Hope you weren't standing there ringing forever, were you?" Not waiting for an answer, she turned quickly on her heels. "Come in, come in."

Suzanne Short was the epitome of her name: a petite woman who looked more like a contemporary of my grandmother from South Dakota than a matron from Manhattan's Upper East Side. A T-shirt with a nautical motif clung snuggly to her swollen stomach. Stiff blonde waves framed her weepy, friendly eyes. She wore large red glasses that were tinted a little too darkly for indoor use.

"Good lord! These pants," she exclaimed, fiddling with her fly. "This zipper does not want to stay up. I simply *have* to take them into the tailor," she remarked to me like an old friend, not a client she was meeting for the first time.

I shrugged and nodded as if I always had the same problem.

"Come into the living room. Let's talk, get to know one another. I can tell you what I have planned for your project."

So this wasn't an office—this was her home. It was a rambling old apartment with lots of tiny rooms, each opening onto another. Windows opened onto landings that overlooked brick walls, making a cross-breeze next to impossible. I was thankful for the air conditioners placed in every room. Similar to the apartments I had seen in countless Woody Allen movies, Suzanne's was cramped, dimly lit, and littered with books. Books were stacked underneath the coffee table, used as end tables, and were precariously collected in the corners of rooms. Suzanne read like an agent.

She motioned for me to take a seat. I gazed at the lumpy faux-rococo-style loveseat covered in plastic. It reminded me of my great-aunt's sofas from Germany, which smelled of moth balls with down filling seeping out of the corners. I sat down with a squeak. "Here, I thought that you might want to take a look at this. It's a *faaabulous* little book. Robin, Robin Leach that is, is a dear old friend of mine. I represented him a few years back on this cookbook."

"Thanks," I said, grasping the thin hardcover book. Robin Leach? Was she kidding me? I glanced around the room, looking for the hidden camera, but the only thing that I saw was a tiny woman fiddling with her fly. By publishing standards, the book was a relic. It was a fetish object filled with recipes by Ivana Trump and tricks for a fabulous backyard barbecue by professional athletes who I had never heard of. I quickly thumbed through the book, then set it on the coffee table next to the porcelain figurines of lap dogs.

"Of course, *your* book would be different." Thank god, I

thought. "This book appeals to a different audience. Your demographic is young, hip, savvy." Okay, I thought, we're sort of on the same page.

I sat back on the worn plastic-covered seat, arms across my chest. I remembered reading an article about body language in a teen magazine that said crossing your arms in front of you says, "Back away. I am a closed-off person!" But so many years later, it was a posture I often found myself assuming. To me, it was warm and nurturing. I was able to cradle my right arm as if it were in a sling. And maybe, just maybe, people wouldn't notice its stillness. Suzanne didn't seem to as she prattled on.

"Suzanne?"

"Yes, dear?"

"Well . . . I guess there is something we should talk about." Here we go, I thought. The subject that I never *wanted* to speak about but always needed to be addressed.

"What's that?"

"Well, you probably noticed that I'm sort of, well, I'm sort of disabled," I explained, using the word *disabled* for lack of a better choice.

"Yes, I noticed," Suzanne said nonchalantly. Is she really being so nonchalant or is her flippancy a method to mitigate this uncomfortable situation? I wondered whether to continue.

"I have a partial paralysis," I said, gesturing with my left hand at my limp right side. I looked over at Suzanne, desperate to read her body language, but all I saw was an elderly woman adjusting the hem of her T-shirt. I waited for some sort of response; now it was my turn to fiddle with the hem of my dress.

Suzanne nodded. That was all I got, an aloof gesture? Well, if that was how my news was received, I certainly didn't need to address it any further.

"Will that be a problem for you or for the book?" I asked.

"I don't see why. You wrote all of the recipes, didn't you?" Now it was my turn to nod. "I don't see how your . . . your situation"—Suzanne paused; she was pleased with this choice of words—"will affect how I sell your book."

"Okay then," I remarked.

"Fine then."

And that was that. There was a part of me that was disappointed. There was a large part of me that never wanted to address what had happened to me physically, to leave it behind, like a forgotten lunch bag. But there was also a conflicting voice, this tiny whisper that would not be forgotten. If I listened to it closely, it reminded me that life didn't always fit neatly into boxes. And this part of me, the one-armed girl who hobbled rather than glided, needed to be acknowledged. It was the new me who had written a cookbook, who had ran a catering company, and who had now traveled to New York. I was actually beginning to come to terms with the person who I had developed into. I thought back to that Scrabble game with David and how I desperately had wanted to swap tales of disability with him. He wouldn't play the trading game with me; that had forced me to answer questions for myself. And here was Suzanne, who wasn't even going to ask me why I walked with a limp or why my right arm crookedly hung limp beside me. This was my agent, the person who was supposed to know me well, to fight for me when needed, and she didn't seem interested in getting to know *me*. At that moment, I made up my mind only to tell her what she asked about—which wasn't much. My agent had made my physicality seem inconsequential. Part of me was happy to not address this, but part of me wondered how we could not. I knew that what I needed was a bit of time and a bit of space in this city of more than eight million people to mull over the events of the day.

"Jen?"

"Oh, hi, A! How's New York?"

"Um, fine?" Once out of Suzanne's "office," I felt a rush of panic. Brian had been looking at apartments all morning, so I called my sister.

"That sounds convincing. What's up?"

"So I met with Suzanne, and . . ."

"And what?"

"And I don't know about her," I said. "She's older than I thought, and I'm not sure if she gets it." I had been looking for an agent for quite some time. Some authors say that it's easier to get a book published than it is to find an agent, a sentiment I was starting to believe. I queried everyone in the business: big agencies with flashy Web sites, individual agents whose names I got from lists that I found online, independent agencies with no Web sites at all. I would query certain agents, never to actually hear from them. And I had gotten close, tailoring my book to different people's specifications, only to be ultimately left out of the publishing game. It seemed that I was destined to watch from the sidelines. And then Suzanne came along. Brian now had Columbia, and I wanted to be at that next step, too;

having an agent was one step closer to getting my cookbook published.

I'm not even sure how I found her. There was such a bevy of to-send piles, haven't-heard-froms, and rejections that when Suzanne's e-mail came floating into my inbox, I jumped on it immediately. This was it! I found an agent! After a solid year of rejections and false starts, I was ready to start hearing from publishers.

I must admit, I was somewhat surprised by Suzanne's advanced age when I met her. In this Internet age of e-mail and IMing, Suzanne's fingers had been nimble. She popped off cheery e-mails to me in California, keeping me updated on "my project." So, when a little, very mature woman answered the door on that warm summer day, let's say I was taken aback. Her bleached blonde helmet head didn't inspire confidence. I had imagined Suzanne as a smart, independent thirty-something. Together we would plot out the best course for my book, turning the world of cookbook publishing on its ear.

"Do you know Robin Leach, that fatuous host of *Lifestyles of the Rich and Famous,* has a cookbook? Or, maybe I should say, had—I'm sure it's out of print by now. Well, I do. Suzanne was his agent, and that's the direction she sees for my cookbook." There was silence on the other end of the line. "Jen, are you still there?"

"Yeah, yeah. I don't know what to say . . . I'm sure you'll be fine."

"Listen," I said with a sigh. "I'm supposed to meet Brian. We still have to find a place to live."

"Okay. And don't worry. You have to learn to compartmentalize; you still have a lot to do in New York."

"You're right. I'll talk to you later; hopefully with apartment news." I closed my cell phone, checked my watch, and shoved my arm upward like the Statue of Liberty holding her torch. A cab came swerving to a stop. I climbed into the backseat; I couldn't face the subway again after my morning with Suzanne.

CHAPTER 18

Apricot Galette

To me, eating seasonally is a no-brainer. Food tastes better when it is grown locally. An apricot grown in December in Chile will not be juicy and flavorful when it reaches the United States. But when summer arrives, the only thing I want to eat is fruit. Sweet, perfumey fruit with delicate fuzzy skin the color of a sunset. Apricots were always the first to hit the market in California, but in New York they come to market with the other stone fruits.

In addition to eating them out of hand, I love to cook with them. I use the word cook loosely, because I find that the less you do with this fruit (as is true with many summer fruits), the better. I love a good pie, syrupy and sugar-kissed, but I will admit, they can be a bit daunting to prepare. Galettes, however, are anything but. Rustic and free-form, once you get the hang of them, you will want to make them all of the time. The dough recipe can be doubled (and even tripled), and freezes like a dream. This galette features apricots, but feel free to try any filling you like, even berries.

FOR THE PASTRY DOUGH:
1 cup all-purpose flour
1 tablespoon sugar
¼ teaspoon baking powder
¼ teaspoon salt
4 tablespoons cold unsalted
   butter, cut into ½-inch pieces
3 tablespoons sour cream
ice water (if needed)

FOR THE GALETTE:
3 cups apricots, cut into sixths
   or eighths (7–8 apricots)
¼–⅓ cup sugar, depending on
   the sweetness of the apricots
1 vanilla bean, scraped of
   interior seeds
Juice of 1 lemon
1 tablespoon flour
1 tablespoon unsalted butter

In a food processor, combine the flour, sugar, baking powder, and salt and pulse until mixed. Add the butter, one piece at a time, and pulse until the mixture resembles coarse sand. Chill the work bowl for 15 minutes.

Place the work bowl in the processor and add the sour cream, pulsing until the dough just comes together. Depending on the weather and humidity, you may need to add ice water, 1 tablespoon at a time, until the dough comes together. Gather the dough, press gently to create a circle, wrap in plastic wrap, and refrigerate for at least 30 minutes before rolling out.

Preheat the oven to 400°F. On a lightly floured surface, roll the dough into a rough circle, measuring about 14 inches. Place on an ungreased baking sheet and set aside.

Slice the apricots, putting them in a medium-size bowl. Taste the fruit for sweetness to determine how much sugar will be needed. In a small bowl, toss the sugar with the seeds from the vanilla bean. Reserve the empty pod for another use. Add the vanilla-sugar mixture and the lemon juice to the apricots, tossing well to coat.

Sprinkle the flour onto the rolled-out dough, leaving a 1-inch border. Place the fruit on top of the flour, leaving the border naked. Fold over the border, pressing gently to secure the dough.

You should have a free-form tart. Dot the surface of the galette with the butter.

Bake for approximately 40 minutes. If the galette appears to be browning too quickly, cover with foil and continue the baking process. Remove from the oven and leave on the baking sheet for 10 minutes to cool, then transfer to a rack to cool completely. The galette is good served as is, but it is wonderful with a dollop of crème frâiche.

serves 6–8

Food to Go

It is amazing to me that all you really need is a little nook of your own personal space in order to feel entirely alone. My little nook was the backseat of that New York City yellow cab, overpoweringly scented by an incense-fragranced car air freshener. As I pressed my back against the sticky vinyl seats, the sweat that had collected on the lining of my summer dress became cool as it mingled with the chill of the recycled air-conditioning. I wanted to close my eyes for a moment to think. But as the car zoomed across town to the west side, the brief journey through Central Park under a canopy of leaves was truly beautiful. I sat, pressed against the door of the taxi, peering out the window and nervously checking the meter. The endless ticking of cents and dollars made me nervous. Was this how time was counted in New York? Were minutes the equivalent of dollars?

The taxi driver was a masterful multitasker: making hairpin turns, swerving around pedestrians, stopping on a dime only inches

227

behind the bumper of the preceding car, all the while talking on a headset, keeping his hands free to wildly gesticulate at careless drivers. We came screeching to a stop, and I was jarred from my reverie long enough to toss the fare through the sliding Plexiglas window and emerge from the cab, straightening my dress that was starting to look as wrinkled with wear as I felt. I had barely closed the door behind me when the cab took off with a squeal.

WE EACH MET on opposite corners of 103rd and Amsterdam. Brian, me, and a shifty-eyed broker named Lou. Meeting on street corners was something that I would get better at once we lived in New York a while, but this was the first clandestine meeting. There were four corners of 103rd and Amsterdam. At which was I supposed to stand? North, south, east, west—I needed concise directions. Finally, I just picked one. Of course, Brian picked another, and the impatient Lou picked another still. Eventually, we all met at the fourth unattended corner for a stressful date with New York City real estate.

"So, I have to say, given your price range and where you want to live, the market's tight," whined Lou. "But there are *some* places I know about, so let's hit it. I have some more clients with a little more wiggle room price-wise that I'm supposed to meet later on today."

Way to make us feel comfortable, Lou. This broker business was entirely new to me. Paying someone else to find you an apartment to *rent* who wasn't even your *landlord*? It all seemed like a racket, but Brian and I were pressed for time. We needed a place to live, and fast. With Lou proclaiming us to be last on his list, he took off practically running—well, jogging—to the first apartment. Brian glanced at me and assertively strode behind Lou, and I, not so assertively, hobbled along behind Brian, bringing up the rear. If you squinted hard, blurring your vision, we almost looked like the Beatles album cover to *Abbey Road*.

"Come on, guys. We have a lot to see and not a lot of time to do it!" beckoned Lou. I looked at Brian, my eyes getting larger, pleading with him to say something.

"Um, Lou, it takes my wife a little longer." Lou glanced behind him, watching me limp to catch up.

"Oh, geez! I'm sorry! Aah, you know, I have a cousin who's a cripple. Yeah, she got in a real bad car accident when we were teenagers. Crushed her legs into I don't know how many pieces. She walks with those special crutches. Her legs don't really work right. But you know what, she's married now, lives a happy life up in Plattsburgh." Lou took a moment, "So, what happened to you?"

I gave my standard reply reserved for people who seemed in too much of a hurry to understand what an AVM was: "You know what, it's a really long story."

A cripple? Is that what I was to some people? I often wondered. When people look at me, what do they see? There are some people, the self-absorbed ones, who I can't imagine see much of anything. They are thankfully too consumed with *their* lives to notice much of what is going on with the rest of the world. But negotiating my body is a strange endeavor. I have tried to make a full recovery as much for me as for other people. I fear their judgment, their questioning glances, their pity.

I don't think of myself in absolutes; therefore, I don't really think of myself as disabled. I try not to think in those terms—

save for the times that I am in a crowded parking lot and see rows of pristine open wheelchair parking spots. *Then* I will whip out my wheelchair parking placard, proclaiming to the world I am a disabled human being. But I would hardly be the next spokeswoman for the disabilities movement. Frankly, I just want to be left alone. I think that's what irks me the most about being seen as disabled; there is absolutely nowhere to hide. In my years of physical therapy, perfecting my gait, attempting to let my arm swing naturally at my side, it was about having an ease and fluidity of movement as much as it was obtaining anonymity. There are few moments when I feel that I can entirely assimilate. My right foot slaps the pavement noisily as I walk by, and sometimes I wish that I could relax into the recesses.

"So, the first apartment is being worked on currently—new paint, some new fixtures. The usual. But it will be done in August," Lou told us, lifting the brim of his trucker-style cap to wipe the perspiration from his forehead. Now that we had all addressed my "disability," Lou had become increasingly solicitous. His nature had softened and his voice had grown louder, as if Brian and I were tourists from a foreign land. "It's on the second floor, and the building's a walk-up. Is that going to be a problem for you?"

"No. I think I can handle it." Little did Lou know I had been up and down subway stairs all morning.

"So, here we are. Feel free to look around. I'm going to make a few calls out here in the hallway."

Brian pushed the door open with a creak and we stepped into the apartment. To say that it was a dilapidated disaster was putting it mildly. Never one to be able to hide anything on my face, my cheeks lost all of their flush, my mouth tasted like cotton, and my eyes were huge.

"Feel free to look around? At what?" I asked, turning to Brian.

The apartment was small, as was to be expected. It was a large square divided into four equally small rooms. The interior walls were incomplete, rising from the tired floorboards and reaching toward the ceiling, though never quite grasping it. The wood floors were filled with dust particles, and grime was held securely between each slat. Fluffy dust bunnies collected in the corners of each room, spots of unknown matter were crusted on the dingy walls, and large red X's were painted messily on the windowsills, which were protected by sturdy metal bars. "So, Lou, what's the deal with these large X's painted everywhere?" Brian called to our broker.

"Oh, they're marking lead paint. Don't worry. That will be painted over before you move in."

"With what? More lead paint, I suppose," I whispered to Brian. I took a look in the "kitchen." It was bare bones to say the least. An industrial-style kitchen sink with a small built-in drying rack stood underneath the two rows of "kitchen" shelves that reminded me of the industrial shelving I had proudly installed in my bedroom in college: L brackets, with a plank of wood resting on top. A mismatched refrigerator stood shyly in the corner, probably in disgust, given the vile odor emanating from the contents left by the previous renter. The exposed pipes from the sink—no counters here—slowly leaked an oily brown liquid.

There was a rumble, then a flushing noise coming from another floor in the building that reminded me to be sure to take a look at the bathroom. I'm glad that I did. Small spaces I can handle, especially after actually living in New York City, but smeary, wretched filth is another thing altogether. The bathroom's dim fluorescent bulb blinked into recognition, its metallic light harshly displaying the room's contents. A tiny six-inch square sink dripped water, echoing the less-than-subtle dripping coming from the kitchen sink. An ocher bathtub streaked with indelible grime and mildew so thick you could scratch your fingernail through it sighed deeply, as if it, too, was ashamed of its own filth. Sitting atop the linoleum floor was an avocado green toilet with a peeling wooden toilet seat. As Brian and I peered inside the toilet bowl to catch a glimpse of the rings, marking age like the rings of a tree, I saw one lone cigarette butt, bloated and decaying in the water. "Okay, I've seen enough," I exclaimed. "Remember what Gabe told us last night? It's easy to fix up a living room or a bedroom; usually, they require a new coat of paint and some elbow grease, but what can you do with a rented bathroom or kitchen? The appliances are a set package. And this is not a package I'm ready to live with."

"Well, you two, what'd you think?" Lou asked, the dollar signs blinking in his beady eyes.

"I think we need to see some other places. We just started looking; I think it would be a good idea to see what's out there," I said as subtly as I could.

"Okay, but you're not going to find anything comparable in terms of size for this price in this neighborhood."

"Well, we can look elsewhere. Why don't you show us what you have?"

Lou shrugged and then lumbered down the stairs. Brian barreled down after him. And I, once again, brought up the rear.

When the day started out, I had been proud of myself for successfully endeavoring the subway. I had ridden it, transferred lines a few times, unassisted, made my way under- and aboveground, and figured my way around the Upper East Side, all before noon. It wasn't as if I wanted some sort of medal, but I had wanted to bask in my pride for a moment. By the end of our seemingly endless afternoon with Lou, I cursed the subway stairs.

I had been jostled, bumped, pushed aside, scooted around, and run into one too many times to count. My voice grew rough with too many "excuse me's" uttered, and I finally stopped apologizing. We stood on the corner of 168th and Broadway, and I wanted to stoop down, bracing myself on my knees, like I had just completed an obstacle course. But there was no time for that. Slowly we crawled our way up Manhattan, ringing bells for supers, who often seemed surprised that the building had any vacancies. But Lou was aggressive. He stood, it seemed, ringing bells for a living. And when he wasn't ringing bells, he was on his cell phone making appointments to ring bells.

The apartments we saw that day got progressively cleaner and larger, the farther uptown we got. But the city wasn't like I imagined Manhattan to be. I came to learn that there is an entire section of this dense city that is forgotten. Manhattan is teeming with people from all walks of life: bankers in their suits, lawyers rushing around with briefs, fashionistas prancing along in stiletto heels, mothers pushing the latest state-of-the-art strollers, and artists with dirt under their fingernails. But there is also another type of Manhattanite: the type who lives in neighborhoods like the one at 168th and Broadway. This is the type of citizen about whom no one ever speaks.

These neighborhood people have lived in New York for decades, have seen it grow and change, and have never truly gotten off the swelling city's shores. They live in ramshackle apartments with generations of extended family. As I walked down these high-numbered streets, it became clear that these aren't just the forgotten places of Manhattan; they are institutionally forgotten. There is no street sweeping, trash collection, or mosaic-laden subway platforms. Slowly, gentrification is taking hold, a leapfrogged landscape of capital and neglect. Brownstones that once had welcoming stoops now have their windows messily boarded up; they slouch next to gleaming metal-and-glass high-rises. Manhattan is tiny. Demand to live on this island outweighs its capacity to house the millions, so developers slowly creep into places that have been forgotten, places where years ago no one ever paid much thought. Yes, Manhattan is changing, but the forgotten remain.

Lou could only feign understanding for so long. He grew impatient of waiting for me to sidestep, one at a time, down the subway stairs, clinging to Brian's sweaty T-shirt for balance. "Aah, listen you two. I got a few phone calls to make, a little bit of running around to do, so why don't I meet you at the final apartment? Okay, just give me a call when you get there. It's fine, just take your time," he said, glancing at me. Then he dashed up the street.

"Let's rest a moment. We should rest." Brian was always understanding. He stood on the corner, shifting his satchel from one side of his back to the other.

"No, no, we can go," I said, trying for the first time that day to be agreeable.

"No. Look, there's a coffee shop across the street. We should sit, collect our thoughts. Let's talk about the apartments we've seen today. And Lou? He can wait." Brian offered his arm to me, and I heavily hooked my arm through his cocked elbow. My back ached, and my now swollen feet were a vibrant fuchsia hue. The city wreaked havoc on my body. I wondered if this was how it was going to be for me in Manhattan. Had Berkeley, with all of its raked curbs, wheelchair-accessible paths, and overly sensitive inhabitants, babied me for years? I had become accustomed to the nurturing, watchful eyes of a progressive college town. In Manhattan, I was faced with a city that I didn't know, that didn't seem to want to know me. "So . . . what are you thinking?" Brian asked, setting an iced coffee in front of me.

I shrugged. "I'm not sure."

"This is what I think—so, the apartments we've looked at way uptown they're clean and huge, but look where we would be living. Do you really want to live next door to Ralph's House of Fried Chicken? Did you even see any markets nearby? You're trying to be a food writer; it seems pretty important to me that we would be living near at least one decent grocery store. The way I see it is this: We're here for only a few years that we know about. We might as well make it worth our while, even if that means we sacrifice size and maybe cleanliness."

"Even if that means taking a huge step down from the type of life that we were living?"

Now it was Brian's turn to do the shrugging. "Even if." Brian reached into his satchel, pulling out his laptop and cell phone.

"This place has wireless. I'm going to check Craigslist, just to see if there's anything new."

"Okay. I'll sit here and wince in pain as I carefully touch the latest blister to appear on my left foot."

"Look at this," Brian said a few moments later. Turning his laptop toward me, I read: One-bedroom apartment, near Columbia University. Close to transportation and the park. Gut renovation. Available August 1st. "I'm going to call." Brian made an appointment for us to see the apartment later that day.

"Wait—what about Lou?" I asked.

"What about him? I'm sure he will understand."

Killing time before our appointment, I dragged Brian on a tour of supermarkets in Morningside Heights, ending up at the Fairway Market in Harlem. "I've heard about Fairway; it's supposed to be like the Berkeley Bowl of New York."

Tucked under the West Side Highway at 132nd and Twelfth Avenue stood an outpost of this popular West Side market. Even at 4:00 P.M. on a Thursday afternoon, it was crowded. I elbowed my way into the market and took my place among the hordes of people in the produce aisles. Produce was expensive. It looked tired from journeying into the city; the three-dollar head of broccoli was wilted, florets crushed from being jostled during travel. I glanced up at the signs telling provenance—many claimed California as their home.

I reached out to gently press a peach, expecting to feel a pleasant give, but what I felt was a solid stone fruit. This peach still needed ripening on the kitchen counter. "I'm feeling a little peckish; I'm going to buy a few apricots for us," I told Brian, plucking a plastic bag from the roll. I selected carefully, picking the softest fruit. I inhaled deeply, hoping to catch a scent of the California summer wafting through. The apricots were little, as I like them to be, with the fruit barely clinging to the stone. We paid and stood outside, under the highway, watching the taxi cabs careen by. I reached into the bag, dusting off a piece of fruit, and took a bite.

"Well, is it everything that you like your apricots to be?" Brian asked, knowing that apricots are my favorite summer fruit.

I chewed carefully, trying to taste the fruit, and I could—but only faintly. It was rather bland, tasting like an apricot that was frozen, its flavor kept a secret. This apricot did not taste like I was eating it in the middle of July. Clearly I was not in California anymore.

"You will never believe the sort of day we have had," I exclaimed to Maia and Gabe. They had come uptown to meet Brian and me for dinner at a French-Caribbean restaurant up the street from our new apartment. Yes, we had found an apartment. In record time according to Maia and Gabe.

"You don't understand; no one finds an apartment in a day in New York City. Your day could have been miserable, but look at what came of it! So . . . tell us all about it," Maia said, sitting back in her chair.

We had all met at dinnertime, which in New York is apparently much later than it is in California. At 8:30, the slim BYOB restaurant on Columbus Avenue was just starting to fill up. I glanced at the brief menu. Clearly it did not change with the seasons. Rich dishes like duck confit with hearty lentil salad were paired with starters of warmed half pears oozing with melted blue cheese, all served on a bed of wilted arugula. Each dish sounded good enough, but after a scorcher of a day, when I could still taste the salty remnants of sweat on my upper lip, the last thing I felt like eating was a cheesy hot pear. Seasonal, seasonal, seasonal was all that I had heard while living and cooking in the San Francisco Bay Area. I had clients who would not hear of melon and prosciutto before the melons were picked at the peak of ripeness in July, juice literally seeping out of their hard exteriors. I wondered what Alice Waters would have to say about me eating a fall fruit in the height of summer?

That night at dinner, I went on and on about our first dizzying day in Manhattan, stopping only to take gulps of wine bought at the corner liquor store and to take a moment to sit back while Brian interjected his thoughts.

In a converted tenement building, on the fourth floor of a five-story walk-up and down a narrow hallway, were the bare bones of what would become our home. The ad had read "gut renovation," although it could have read "large 400-square-foot bathroom," because upon renting the apartment, the bathroom—or at least the bathtub and the toilet—was all that was complete in our little corner of New York. The floorboards were torn up, exposing dusty concrete floors. There were hardly any walls, as they had been torn down to the studs. Tools I did not even recognize were lying about on the floor, awaiting their use the following day. But even in this ultimate state of disrepair, it was the finest apartment we had seen all day. Brian and I had taken a moment to discuss the building; we huddled in the corner next to the pipes that would become the kitchen sink. The landlady who had owned the building for years told Brian and me that the neighborhood had been like a shoot-em-up Wild West show ten years ago.

But now, like much of New York, it, too, was gentrifying. The building was split between large ethnic families and people from the university. Brian could walk to work each day, a novel notion coming from California.

"What do you think?" asked Brian.

"It's definitely the best we've seen . . ."

"But it's on the fourth floor of a walk-up?"

I sighed. "I'll manage. So it's not ideal, but I'll learn. Besides, it's so close to school for you."

"I know, walking distance. You can't beat that."

I nodded.

So we took the apartment. If there is one thing I learned, it's that you have to act fast when it comes to New York City real estate.

"My god, I forgot to ask: How did the meeting with your agent go?" Maia asked later that night on the subway back to her apartment.

"Ugh, I don't even know. That hardly seems like it happened today. Can I tell you about it later?"

That morning I had looked on in amazement at my fellow passengers—real people, in work clothes, napping as if they were home and had hit the snooze button on their alarm clocks—while they were riding the subway. It seemed so unsavory. But that night, I, too, rested my eyes on the subway train like a true New Yorker.

CHAPTER 19

Summer Clafoutis

Summer is as much about days by the pool and walks at twilight as it is about refreshing watermelon and the other luscious fruit of the season. This dessert epitomizes summertime for me—simple, tantalizing, and delicious.

With only a handful of ingredients, clafoutis is not quite a custard, not quite a cake. It is a subtle dessert bursting with summer fruit. This clafoutis came to symbolize both beginnings and endings for me as I wrapped up my life in Berkeley and prepared to make my way to New York.

1 cup summer fruit*	1 cup milk (not skim)
1 tablespoon plus ⅓ cup sugar	2 teaspoons vanilla extract
	pinch of salt
3 large eggs	½ cup all-purpose flour

Preheat the oven to 350°F. Lightly butter a 9-inch pie pan. Arrange the fruit evenly at the bottom. Sprinkle 1 tablespoon of sugar over the fruit and set aside.

Whisk together the eggs and ⅓ cup sugar until smooth and slightly frothy, about 1 minute. Add the milk, vanilla extract, and

*Use almost any summer fruit that you like: sliced apricots, peeled wedges of peaches, berries of all sorts, except for strawberries, which are too watery and turn to mush.

salt, whisking to combine. Sift the flour over the egg mixture and continue to whisk until smooth.

Pour the batter over the fruit in the pie plate. Some pieces of fruit will float and move; disperse them evenly after pouring, if necessary. Bake for 45–50 minutes. Clafoutis will puff up substantially but will fall during cooling. Cool for 30 minutes, then enjoy.

serves 8

The Last Bite

Moving is a trial. I have never been a very good packer, or unpacker, for that matter. It is impossible for me to live neatly from a suitcase. Within minutes of opening, the contents of my bag look as though they have been tumbled in the dryer. When I went to sleepaway camp, I would return home each July with a long list of pen pals' addresses; freshly tie-dyed psychedelic T-shirts; and a suitcase full of dirty clothes. The suitcase would get dragged into my bedroom, set squarely at the foot of my bed, opened, just to take out my latest craft projects, and there it would sit—for days. Each day, my mother would pass my room to check on my progress. There she would find me, lying in that lazy way that only kids on summer break can, on my bed, flipping through a magazine, my suitcase opened yet still full, exactly where I had placed it when I got home.

Days would pass; she would creep into my bedroom, collecting laundry—piles of wadded-up underwear and pajamas covered in a fine coating of camp silt. She would ask me if I had unpacked my suitcase yet, knowing full well what my answer would be. The one-week mark would approach, my suitcase having caused a permanent depression on the carpet in my bedroom, and she would have to call me on my laziness. My mom has no problem unpacking or living out of a suitcase. I do. So you can only imagine my sluggish dismay in packing up our entire life for the past four years in Berkeley in order to make the cross-country move to New York City.

Now in my late twenties, my belongings could be disassembled and packed back into large boxes, but I found myself purging rather than packing many of my things. Paperback novels were sold back to the used bookstores at which I had purchased them. Clothing was pulled from the recesses of my closet and given away. Going through piles of old shoes, I stumbled upon high heels, which years ago I had hoped to wear again. They were now tired and out of fashion but had become symbols of the old me—I couldn't toss them out yet. As I blew dust from the toes and put them in large plastic bags to be placed in storage, I made note of never letting myself completely forget that I once was and could still become an able-bodied person.

The one area that I judiciously packed was the kitchen. Our new Manhattan apartment was going to be drastically smaller than our Berkeley one, and the kitchen was in typical New York fashion—itsy-bitsy. I would have two overhead cabinets to place all of my plates, bowls, glasses, and other sorts of kitchen gadgets. Packing up the contents of my kitchen shelves was especially difficult. I had three piles: the going, the storage, and the giveaway. As I took each glass from the cabinet, crystal clear and cleanly squeaking, I weighed my options. Dishes were placed in the storage pile. I sighed as I wrapped each piece in paper, newsprint covering the bright patterns of my grandma's teacups. The handles were so delicate; I hoped that they would remain intact until I would see them again.

There were empty platters from my catering business, for once not waiting to be filled. Nosheteria Catering was put on hold due to the move. Cooking in my tiny New York kitchen would be too large an undertaking in too enormous a city. The platters sat in the ever-growing giveaway pile.

SOME PEOPLE HAVE summers at the beach, the salt from the air mixed with the salt from the ocean, bleaching the pigment from their hair. Hamburgers are grilled so dark that they look like charcoal briquettes, and hot dogs are cooked so crunchy that their skins literally pop when bitten. There are songs of summertime— tunes that make you want to kick off your flip-flops and move your toes to the music no matter how often you hear them.

Each year, I think that spring *should* arrive in March, and I begin to gear up for the summer produce. I forget that this month merely marks spring's awakening on the calendar. But a mark on the calendar does not necessarily mean a mark in nature. It doesn't matter how old I am or how many winters have shown me differently. I am ready for winter to be complete in March. I wait, saying good-bye to the citrus fruit of those colder months, with their tough peels protecting them from winter's frost. Every week at the market, I peek my head around the corner into the produce section. I close my eyes and breathe in deeply, testing my sense of smell. My nose twitches. I smell the astringency of lemons mixed with the strong perfume of the grapefruit. Again I breathe, concentrating on the juices of an apricot or the slightly sulfuric smell of sweet strawberries, but these are a memory of the fruits of last spring. I open my eyes and see a bevy of citrus, beautiful in its own right, but not what I am longing to see.

Next week, the game begins again, and it will continue until the one day that my nose does not fool me. I peer down the aisles, and there they are, blinking back at me. First come the strawberries, jockeying for space among their friends in the strawberry basket. They are far from perfect, these firsts-of-the-season. Tops a verdant green, shoulders a milky pale, like the head of a bald man who has not seen the sun for months. They look like strawberries, and they taste a bit like strawberries. But these early risers are not at their peak. Just a few short weeks more.

As the strawberries grow juicier, the apricots begin to ripen. Spring has hit! Such a short season in California, it quickly lapses into a long summer. For me, summer marks a wonderful time of year filled with an abundance of fruit in the marketplace. The weather becomes warm, the days long, seeming to stretch on forever. These long days bring reading in the twilight or rising early in the morning to experience the dew crisply evaporating in the first light of day. But that summer, the long days meant making one last trip before nightfall to the storage unit Brian and I had rented in order to cram one more box marked "FRAGILE— kitchen stuff" into a ten-by-ten-foot storage locker.

We would arrive home to our gradually depleting apartment and lay exhausted on the couch. Then I would look over into the kitchen, spotting my large containers of flour waiting to be used, the sugar waiting to sweeten, and vials of vanilla waiting to softly flavor, and I would leap off the couch.

"Where are you going?" Brian would ask.

"We might be packing up the house, I may even be making *some* progress in the kitchen, but there still is so much to do."

"I'll help you pack all of that up. Don't worry."

"I know; it's not the stuff. I still have a lot of ingredients to go through. Look," I said, picking up the flour, "I must have two pounds of flour here. What do you expect me to do with all of this? I can't just throw it away."

And so my desire to use up all that I had purchased in past months led to my making clafoutis. A lot of clafoutis. For me, it was the summer of clafoutis. Who couldn't buy, and subsequently use, eggs and a little bit of milk? I couldn't be kept away from the market with all of the luscious pieces of fruit waiting to be eaten. I would buy a few pieces: peaches with skin so soft they were like a worn tuft of flannel and olallieberries that stained their containers with ripe juices. Making clafoutis couldn't be simpler, and with each eggy dessert made, my rations of flour and sugar dwindled.

NEVER ONE TO keep homemade desserts to myself, I drove yet another clafoutis over to my parents' house. New York would be the first time in my life that my parents would be more than a car ride away. As much as these sojourns were about eating clafoutis, they were also about spending another moment with my mom. She would set the kettle to boil on the stove. As the kettle whistled, my mom poured the steaming water into the teapot, activating the aromatic leaves.

"How's it coming along?" she asked.

"Fine," I replied, gliding the knife into the clafoutis. The baked fruit, slightly crystallized with glistening bits of sugar, broke softly against the pressure of the knife. "It seems rather never-ending, but Brian and I are definitely making some progress. I never thought I was a pack rat. I'm not a pack rat, am I?"

My mom shrugged. "You're nowhere near members of *my* family, but everyone has *stuff*."

Years ago, when my grandmother passed away, it had taken my mom and her siblings months to clean out her house. The drawers in her bathroom were so full of samples and hotel shower caps that they barely closed. The closet in the master bedroom was stocked full of clothes my grandma had never even worn, including several pair of purple trousers of various sizes with the sale tags still in place. Her pantry was overflowing with boxes of rice, dented cans of soup, and bags of flour three-deep—she was always ready to make a pie.

To watch my grandmother bake pies was to witness a miraculous feat of turning nothing into something. Something that only moments ago was a pile of flour, Crisco, and butter would become a smooth and elastic dough waiting to be rolled out and shaped. Into the pan the dough would go, sliced fruit was tumbled in next, and then some aromatics—cinnamon, nutmeg, lemon peel. The filled pie awaited its topping, another sheet of dough. It was then crimped along the edge and baked. Halfway through the process, the house began to fill with a powerful aroma of fruit, cinnamon, and warmth. Peering through the steamy oven window, I would wait, and in the last moments of baking, I watched the pie turn from peaked and moon-baked to crisp and golden brown. Each one of the parts may have been fine on its own, the salty blandness of the crust, the fruit kissed with sweetness from the sugar—but together they were an outstanding achievement. A pie, warm and syrupy from the oven. A transformation.

"You know, A, I think this move is great for both you and Brian," my mom said, her voice trailing off as she took another sip from her milky tea. She swallowed slowly. "But I have to say it makes me a bit nervous."

"Nervous? Why? You knew that it was bound to happen sometime."

"It's just." She paused, choosing her words carefully. "Who will work with you? You know that your therapy is important. Your health is of the utmost importance. I talked to Brian—"

"Wait, what? When?"

"I talked to him a few days ago."

"He never said anything about this to me."

"I asked him not to. This was a conversation between the two of us."

Moving, much like any task that happens to one member of my family, had in turn become a group activity. My mom had made many trips to our storage unit with Brian while I remained at our apartment packing final boxes of books and dishes. It was during one of these fateful trips that my mother had a talk with him. "This is such an exciting move for both you and Adrienne. Really—you're going off to Columbia, and Adrienne is pursuing her cookbook. I couldn't be happier."

Brian nodded.

"But, you know, I have to tell you, it makes me a little concerned."

"Really, why is that?" Brian asked, taking the bait.

"Well, obviously, I can't be there—not that I want to—but you know, Adrienne and I still do quite a bit of her therapy together. I analyze her gait, massage her hand, stretch her out when I can."

"I know that; I help her, too. But she can do a lot of those things on her own as well," Brian said, coming to my defense. "In fact, I think that in the past few years, Adrienne has really shown her independence. I think she's ready to do quite a bit on her own."

"That may be so. But still—you have to promise me something—you have to take care of her."

Brian looked over at the passenger seat, seeing that my mom was serious, with her mouth downturned slightly. "Okay. Of course. I hope you know that I want to take care of your daughter wherever we are living. That's why I married her." But looking over at my mom again, he could only see the back of her head as she peered out the window at the passing cars.

I, however, was not quite as understanding as my husband, furiously remarking, "But it was about me. You had a conversation about me." I hated the idea of a conspiratorial conversation taking place about me, especially when I was perfectly capable of having the conversation myself.

"Well, yes. I made Brian promise to take care of you . . . to look out for you."

I was dumbfounded. "What is this, Mom—the Victorian era?" I could feel myself getting hot, and it had nothing to do with the fact that it was July.

"I am your mother. I have the right to make sure you're cared for."

"Okay. I guess that's fine, but I'm almost thirty years old. When is this going to stop?"

"Probably never. I worry about you, no matter how much you tell me not to."

"But, Mom, I am a capable, thoughtful, remotely happy human being. You have to understand that; sometimes you have to let me be."

"I do. I'm sorry for making you so upset, but I'm not going to apologize for what I have done."

It was so like my mother—stubborn to a fault. Something had happened to her over the past years. I can only imagine what it was like for her. She had lost a part of her husband at a time when the two of them should have been planning the next phase of their lives together. Then, a few short years later, one of her children is felled by an unknown brain malformation. But this overprotection made me feel like the child I never thought I was.

My parents had never been overly protective. In high school, I had friends who had parents so crazed they wanted to meet and know all of their children's friends and parents. If cell phones had been prevalent, I am sure that they would have been calling their semigrown children's numbers continually. Of course, as teenagers are wont to do, those same friends lied through their teeth in order to have one ounce of freedom. My parents were different. They certainly weren't the cool parents. We didn't have a pool table or a big-screen television at our house. But my parents did the unthinkable—they trusted me; and then they let me be. They raised mature, thinking adults in my sister and me.

It wasn't that everything changed when I had my AVM. It

wasn't that my mother was now parenting an entirely different person, but my illness brought on an unforeseen dependency. I had felt like half of a person, and I called on the people around me to come and to fill me up. My mother had filled in so many of the blank parts. But as time went on and I found new ways to fill myself up, through cooking, and writing, new friends and environments, I did not need my mother to come by and fill me up in the same ways anymore. Like a bottomless cup of rich and warm coffee that you keep drinking from, even when you have had too much and are sure to become jittery from the caffeine, my mother was too much of a good thing. She needed to see that it was time for her to stop worrying.

Now it seemed that my mother was the parent of an adolescent child—an adolescent who was married and ready to begin the next phase of her life. "Mom, you have to learn to trust me."

"I do."

"Really? Because when you go sneaking around, making deals with Brian, worrying about my future, it kind of seems like you don't at all."

My mother smirked.

I continued. "You have to understand, all the things that you want for me, the ideal gait, the free use of my right arm, in short, to be close to perfect again—I want all of those things more. But right now, I guess I'm sort of happy with where I am. And I need you to be, too."

I looked over at my mom, who was spinning her soiled fork between her fingers. "Fine. Just promise me that you won't go backward; you have worked so hard."

Typical. I knew that my mom had heard everything that I had

told her, but it would take a while for my words to be processed and then to take effect. "I promise. Listen, I hate to eat and run," I said, gathering my things. "But Brian and I still have a lot to do. Do you know that Brian has forty boxes of books still to be put in storage? Forty boxes!" I said, shaking my head. "Keep the rest of the clafoutis. If I see another slice, I think I'm going to scream. We'll talk later."

Driving home, past the coffeehouse where Brian and I had first met and the bakery with those killer morning buns with their layers of sweet puffed pastry that I would surely miss, I knew that I was finally ready to leave Berkeley.

CHAPTER 20

Black Beans

Not quite a soup but not quite a side dish either, these black beans can be thrown together in no time. It seems that I always have a can or two of black beans in my pantry, and when garnished with freshly diced tomato, a dollop of sour cream, and some cilantro, a nourishing meal can be easily made on the fly. Rich and satisfying, beans like these are what I imagined my neighbors to be simmering when Brian and I arrived at our new home in New York.

1 cup finely diced onion
1 cup finely diced green bell
   pepper
2 tablespoons olive oil
salt and pepper to taste
3 cloves garlic, sliced
¼ teaspoon cayenne pepper

½ teaspoon chili powder
2 teaspoons ground cumin
15-ounce can black beans
1 cup water
1 tomato, chopped
cilantro, coarsely chopped
sour cream

In a medium-size saucepan, over medium heat, sauté the onion and pepper in the olive oil until the onion becomes translucent, 5–6 minutes. Season with salt and pepper. Add the garlic and continue to sauté until the onion begins to brown. Add the cayenne pepper, chili powder, and cumin, toasting until fragrant, about 1 minute.

Add the beans, undrained, and 1 cup of water. Bring to a boil. Turn the heat down to low and simmer for 15 minutes, until the flavors begin to meld. Season with salt and pepper and garnish with tomato, cilantro, and sour cream.

serves 4 for a side dish, 2 for an entrée

Home Cooking

It is said that every major city is best seen from a specific vantage point. Reyner Banham said Los Angeles is best seen from the freeway; the wide multilane highways parallel this sprawling city. New York, I think, is best seen from rooftops, where you feel unencumbered and free. The tar-covered tops give a glimpse of how many people live in New York. Peel back those roofs, and you might get to see how people actually live. As the 747 hovered over JFK, I gazed out the window into the night sky lit by millions of bright lights. In moments, this bird's eye view would become my reality. It would no longer appear peaceful and calm, as I would be plunged into the dizzying depths of all that New York had to offer.

The buildings that moments ago were miniscule dots on the horizon grew large and life-size. We landed in New York. There was no Maia, no Gabe to meet us at the airport. No celebratory hug of recognition from friends. Celebration was not necessary;

we were home now. Our suitcases landed with a thud on the meandering path of the baggage claim, before Brian wrestled them from the carousel. The rest of our belongings were either safe in a storage unit in Berkeley not to be seen or thought of for at least two years or they were on a moving truck being transported across the United States. The pieces of our life fit together like a wall of Legos, following us in our cross-country move. They would arrive in New York weeks later. We had packed little more than what a person brings on summer vacation for those first weeks in New York. Save for the bath towels and jumbles of bedclothes tucked into a small suitcase, Brian and I had the look of holiday travelers.

We waited in the taxi line outside the terminal, ignoring the men standing around, softly whispering, "Where do you want to go?" and "Taxi into the city, forty dollars." The heat was oppressive. I looked around the taxi line, and there was a man taking a handkerchief from his pocket to blot the salty sweat from his reddening face. Children were having meltdowns, tired of being shuttled about all day and told to hurry up, then wait. Airplane travel can be inhumane—people crammed closely together, like at a nightclub without the pulsating techno music. I felt like one of those tired children; I longed to crawl onto the luggage cart that Brian was pushing, making it my stroller in the taxi line. But I would be good and wait my turn like the adult I told my mother I was a few days ago.

The line inched on until we got a cab. Telling the driver where we were heading, he swerved onto the highway and began to make the drive to our new home. Through the years, the drive to the airport and then home again had been the same. I had lived

within a forty-mile radius all my life. I knew where the gas sta-
tions were, the twenty-four-hour quick-marts, the Chinese restaurants, and the coffee shops. Now there was an entirely new
drive home to make, and not only was it entirely new, but I would
not even be the one driving. New York was a city of taxis; it was
up to the driver to know where you lived and to bring you home
safely. Our driver was swift, talking into a headset at a pace that
mirrored his driving. He made his way from highway, to side
streets, to major thoroughfares, until finally we arrived on the
west side of Manhattan. Our new neighborhood looked different tonight. The heat had driven the neighbors outdoors. Families had set up sunken beach chairs on the sidewalk. People were
firmly planted on front stoops like their rear ends were made for
that bit of pavement, and kids rode their mini-scooters up and
down the blocks.

"Up there is fine, right-hand side of the street," Brian told the
taxi driver as we slowed to a stop. I got out of the cab, curb side,
and waited for Brian and the cab driver to unload the suitcases
from the trunk. As the three of us stood in the street in this huge
city, Brian paid the fare, and I wondered what the driver thought.
Did he know that we were coming home for the very first time?
Did he think we had more of a reason to be in New York than
he did? Brian put his hand on my back, and I shifted, the heat
making me not really wanting to be touched. "Are you ready?
Let's go up."

A simple brick building, it was crammed together with the
other brick buildings on the street, jostling for space on the corner. Brian turned the key in the ornate iron front door. I stood
in front of the door, holding it open as he lugged each one of our

bags inside. I, too, stepped inside, the heavy door wheezing closed behind me. As the door clicked closed, I looked at the handle and smirked. Engraved on it were the letters P-U-S, a lopped-off imperative of the word PUSH, telling you exactly how to get out of the building if you were so inclined.

When Brian had asked if I was ready to go up, he was not asking so in the figurative sense. With our new apartment on the fourth floor of a five-story walk-up, it seemed hard for me to believe that a few years ago I was in a wheelchair. "You lead the way; it may take me a while longer," I said, stepping aside as Brian's scrawny arms grasped the handles of the suitcases.

"Well then, see you up there."

I grasped the handrail with my left hand and steadied myself on the narrow stairway by leaning on my closed right fist. This was an old building. The stairs were steep and shallow, and they seemed to pitch forward in a rickety way. I began my upward climb. I could hear Brian in the distance, one flight away—boom, boom, step, boom, boom, step, the suitcases leading the way up the dim stairway. My climb was different, unencumbered by bags yet still measured—step, pause, step, pause, taking one stair at a time.

It was late evening, yet the building showed no signs of going to sleep. Behind closed doors I could hear children yelling to their siblings in foreign languages. From the pleading cries, it was clear that someone was unhappy. I breathed deeply; I could almost see sliced onions frying on the stove in a dusty iron skillet. The smell permeated the air, resting as heavily as a herd of dozing elephants. As I rounded the corner of the landing to the third floor, I stood a little straighter and thought, I can do this—only one more flight to go. On this last flight, the stairs lay in front of me crooked, not pitching forward, but rather side to side, as if an invisible fat man had set up his camp on one side. This floor smelled different, with the piquant smell of green peppers drifting lazily through the air. The vegetal haze was spicy yet sleepy all at once. There was a heavy, musty note in the background, possibly of black beans simmering away on the stove, offering an inexpensive sustenance in a city that is ruled by cost. It seemed that I lived in a building of cooks.

The fourth floor finally came, and not a step too soon. Across the dingy linoleum tiles at the end of the hallway stood our apartment. Brian had left the door ajar. I was anxious to see what our gut renovation would be. I pushed open the door and peeked my head around the doorjamb. "Well?" I called to Brian. The lights were still off and Brian was in the bedroom, setting our bags down.

"I waited for you. Should we turn the lights on together?" The apartment was dim, but without blinds to shut out the lights of the city, it was hardly dark. I could make out the outline of a row of appliances in the kitchen. The refrigerator, clicking and humming away, stood next to a mini-stove. Let's say there would be no roasting of a twenty-pound Thanksgiving turkey this year, not that I even knew enough people in this city to invite over to eat a twenty-pound bird. Next to the ministove was the kitchen sink, gleaming stainless steel—and that was all. There was no counter, no place to do hours of careful cutting while longing for the complete use of both of my hands to make the process seamless and quick. Brian flicked on the lights. There it was—broad open space. With the wood floors stained and the short walls white, holding the ceiling back from smothering us, our apartment was a closed box awaiting our things to make it home.

An empty apartment can be either inspiring—a blank slate on which to build your life—or it can be intimidating—filling your life again can be a daunting task. I remembered feeling trepidation when Brian and I had first moved in together in Berkeley. As I stared at that apartment, it seemed so cavernous, like an echo could be achieved by dropping a coin on the floor. But in New York, with Brian by my side, I was ready to start my life all over again, and in a sense, to reinvent myself. I was ready to stop dwelling: on hospitals, on therapy, on comparisons to the girl I used to be. It was not that I would ever forget those aspects of my life, but I was ready for them to be reminiscences, stories I would tell that would start with the sentence, "I used to . . ." We had asked the landlady to let in a delivery person, who had brought us a fold-out sofa. This valuable couch-cum-dining-table-cum-bed would be our only piece of furniture in the apartment for the next several days until our belongings arrived from California. The sofa sat starkly alone in the center of the empty living room. I began to laugh. "It's sort of like we're camping."

"When have *you* ever been camping?" Brian chortled.

"Okay, let me rephrase that. It's sort of how I imagine camping to be."

The temperature of the apartment was similar to the hot August night outside. For the first time since entering, I felt the stifling heat, like a low oven with the door shut to keep the hot air in. If walls could sweat, these would have. In an attempt to make myself at home in this echoey space, I dropped my purse with a thump next to me on the wooden floor. Pushing my sweaty shoes off my feet, I stood barefoot on the apartment floor. The floor and walls were covered with a barely visible layer of dust, and I imagined burly workmen, sporting utility belts and carpenter jeans encrusted with spackle, tromping through the apartment only days before.

"Should I open the windows, try to get some sort of cross-ventilation going?" Brian said, stepping around the sofa to the windows.

I nodded. "First thing tomorrow—air conditioner." Some sort of cooling device was definitely needed. I could feel myself wilting and the gentle warmth of northern California summers vanishing.

Brian heaved the window upward, opening our world in the little apartment to the outdoors. Even on the fourth floor, New York City was far from silent. The clucking of women in the street, their voices mixing with the salsa music blaring out of battery-operated stereos on the corner, and the low rumble of the cars below punctuated by the honking of horns—this was my new soundtrack. I walked over to the window, gazing out, adjusting to my new surroundings, looking down at the clusters of people, some scurrying home, others stopping to chat with their neighbors.

"I'm not tired yet; are you?" I asked Brian.

"Not really. Should we go out?"

"Yeah, I guess we should. It's not as if we have anything keeping us in our empty apartment."

"Okay then, let's go explore."

I slipped on my shoes once again and made my way to the

front door. Brian locked up and in the hallway turned to me and asked, "Do you need a hand going downstairs?" his outstretched hand beckoning to me.

"No, I think I should be able to manage." Brian barreled down the stairs, and slowly I took them, one step at a time.

Epilogue

It was early autumn in New York. Brian had just started teaching at Columbia, and our tiny apartment on the fourth floor was already beginning to fill up. The couch sat looming in the corner of the living room, my desk was wedged into place, and the kitchen cabinets were bursting at the seams, as if we had lived in that apartment for years. I had spent my time wandering the city, each day picking a new neighborhood to explore and hoping to find some new coffee shop or market. But my cell phone was always poised, awaiting that life-changing telephone call from my agent telling me that she had sold my cookbook. What I got was another sort of telephone call.

"I'm sorry, dear, that's just the way the cookie crumbles. We tried."

Silence.

"Hello, hello," Suzanne said, not frantically but rather impatiently.

"Yes. I'm here."

"So we tried. But as they say, time is money, and I just can't put any more time into your project."

Each of Suzanne's idioms was one too many. "Time is money" made me feel like a commodity, but I guess in Suzanne's world, that's what my cookbook was. It was *my* labor of love, but to her it was potential dollar signs. I knew that this was a tough business, but after writing an entire book, finding an agent, shopping my book around, and almost getting it published, I still felt like a babe in the woods. This couldn't be the end of the story, could it?

For the first time in years, I didn't know what to do with myself. The prospect of the cookbook had dissolved, the catering business was no longer, and the question of what to do with each day lay before me, endless and unanswered. I felt entirely voiceless. Each morning, Brian would awake and head off to Columbia, his time occupied with teaching and colleagues. My days were still spent wandering the vast city, but now the cell phone was tucked away, and the wanderings became aimless, dejected. I had read how New York could be one of those places that chews you up and spits you out and, I just felt like a piece of cud.

Moving east made me aware just how much of a California girl I was. I was temporarily lost without Berkeley Bowl and Monterey Market, but it wasn't long before I found the Union Square Greenmarket, its stalls overflowing with locally grown produce. The man in fingerless gloves selling piles of potatoes was quick with a greeting and a recipe suggestion. It wasn't the to-and-fro of conversation with my fellow shoppers in Berkeley, but it was surely beneficial.

As fall transitioned to winter, I thought of Octobers in California, where I would serve roasted butternut squash with balsamic glaze and shavings of salty Parmesan cheese—even if we were experiencing a particularly warm autumn and the nectarines were still hanging on. Now, gazing out my window with Central Park in the distance, the leaves beginning to dapple in an array of fiery tones, the nectarines were long forgotten, and those firm winter squash were all I could find at the market. My roasting pans were readily put to use. I learned the meaning of eating seasonally in a place that actually had seasons.

The anonymity of the city had become refreshing. As the bustle swirled around me, I realized that people wondered about me only as much as I wondered about them. They didn't know me before my AVM—my past had been effaced. But so were my accomplishments; I was simply another writer and food lover in a city crawling with them.

Winter arrived like a flurry, and with the cold weather came a much needed visit from an old friend. Nolan had been Brian's best friend in high school and was now a writer, one who had endured years of disappointment before hitting his stride.

The three of us were out to lunch, sharing a New York–style pizza that was quite different from the soggy pizza casserole I was presented with at Vallejo. Thin crust, with pure tomato sauce splattered on the surface, it looked like a deflated rubber ball. And I felt pretty deflated, too, as I told Nolan about my troubles in New York. Nolan took a bite from the crackly, charred crust, and said, "So I was thinking, Adrienne, you should write a memoir. I mean, it's not every day that someone meets a cook who had an AVM." He took another slice. "And who knows? It'd probably be good for you."

As he chewed, I ruminated. Nolan was right—it was good for me. Writing a cookbook had helped me discover what I love to do but it had also allowed me to obscure my disability. But writing a memoir gave me nowhere to hide; it forced me to own up to my life. Sometimes another person's words tell you exactly what you should have been telling yourself. It was Lucy's suggestion to concretize my love for the kitchen in the form of a cookbook, which eventually led to Nolan's suggestion to write a memoir. Thank goodness for the good ideas of good friends.

I began to pour over old recipes from the cookbook. For others, they were simply lists of ingredients, but for me each recipe held a memory—of people, of events, of trials—from the last few years. What was missing was the story behind each recipe. A German-Style Potato Salad with Asparagus was more than a side dish; it captured a moment from a fateful dinner. An Apricot Galette was not just dessert but a reminder of summer—the summer spent in Vallejo, the summer move to Berkeley, and now humid summers in New York. I realized that there was a book to be written, exposing the interior beneath the recipes. This was enough to make me sit down at my computer and begin to write my story.

Soon, my days in New York started to resemble my days in California. In the evenings, Brian would come home from Columbia, assume the position of sous chef, and we would prepare dinner together. We would talk about our days, his filled with music and students, mine filled with words and food. And invariably, after the dishes, had been done, I would call home to check in with my family. My mother and I would swap stories. She would listen as I told her about my latest cooking triumph, and I would listen with envy as she told about the obscene selection of tomatoes available at Monterey Market. Our topics of conversation had changed from my gait and the state of my hand to the busyness of my life in the city and her life in California. We rarely would talk about my therapy, and that turned out to be the best therapy of all.

Acknowledgments

I **never thought I** would write a memoir, but I am so glad that I did. It helped me to clarify aspects of my life; and, of course, certain people, whether they are characters in this book or lovely characters in my life, stand out as playing a central part in my story.

This book would never have been completed without my husband, Brian—a constant support, a font of ideas, a reader with a critical eye, one who is there with a quick laugh, and one who always has a hunger for my food.

To my parents, Michael and Karen Handler—what an intricate balance that has arisen among all of our lives. Dad, I write this to you not truly knowing if you will understand—you led a life of love, respect, and understanding, by example. Each day, I find myself trying to do the same. Mom, your strength and wisdom know no bounds; I am continually amazed by you. To Jennifer, through miles and time zones, one thing will always remain the same—you are my confidante and my best friend.

To my agent, Emmanuelle Alspaugh, thank you for spotting a diamond in the rough in this book; your guidance has been inspirational. For Cara Bedick, my editor, your mindful edits, generous support, and thought-provoking critiques brought this book to life.

To Sarah Kleinman and Zachary Sharrin, who have been there from the very beginning, thank you for your friendship. Rolin Jones, great ideas are shared over pizza; let me know when I can be of assistance to you. Bruce and Ellen Kane, Debbie Kane, Eugenio Messina, Leonard Bullock, and Nishka Chandrasoma, thank you all for your love and encouragement. And lastly, to anyone who has eaten a meal at my house, whether it was a success or a flop, I thank each of your eager stomachs.

Printed in the United States
By Bookmasters